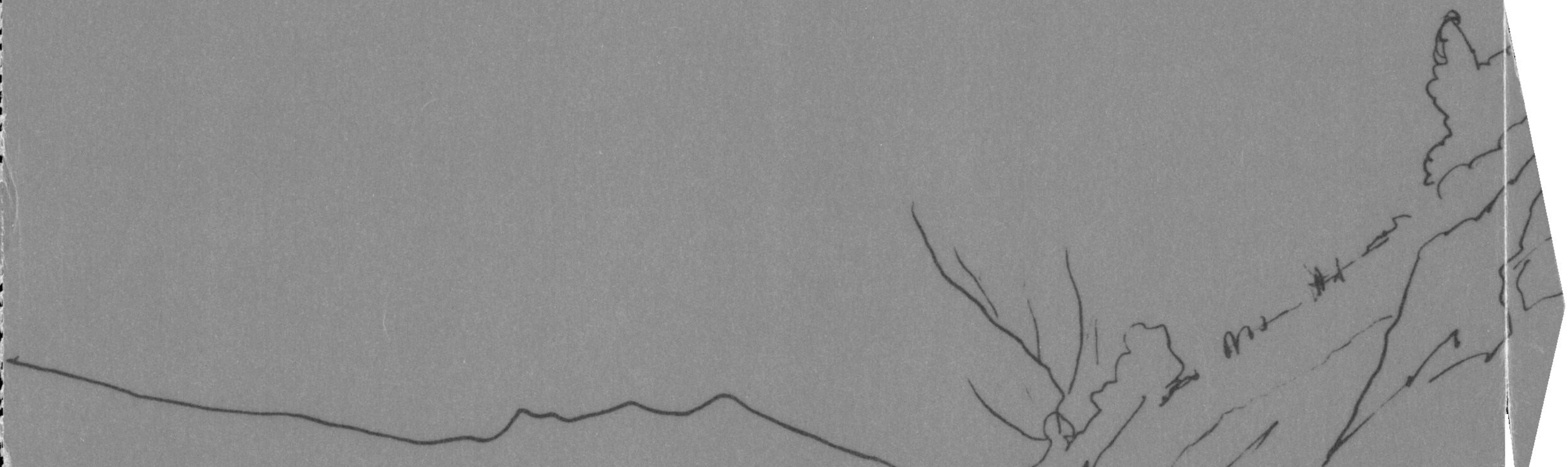

1

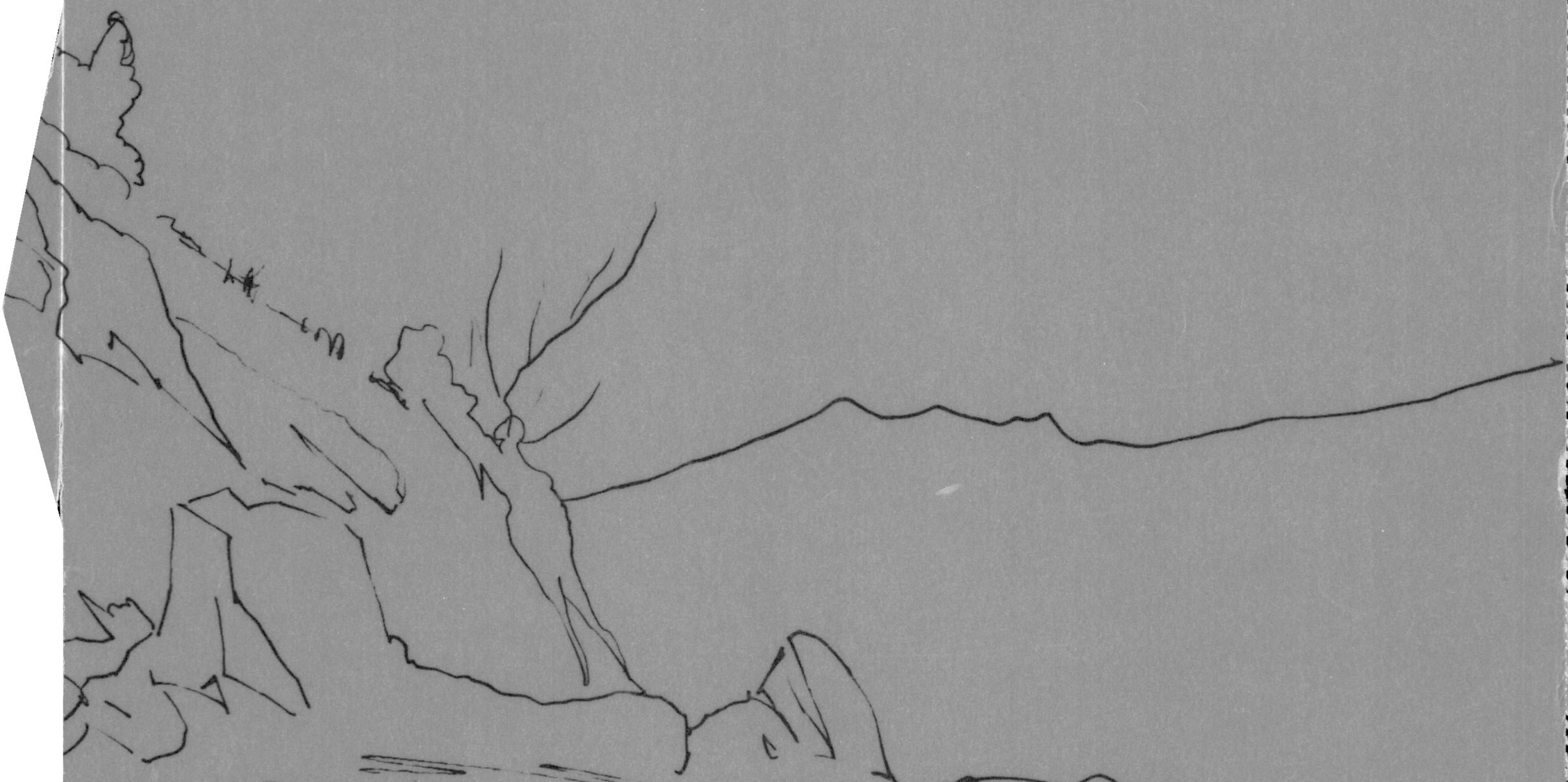

READY TO PAINT

Hills & Mountains

Arnold Lowrey

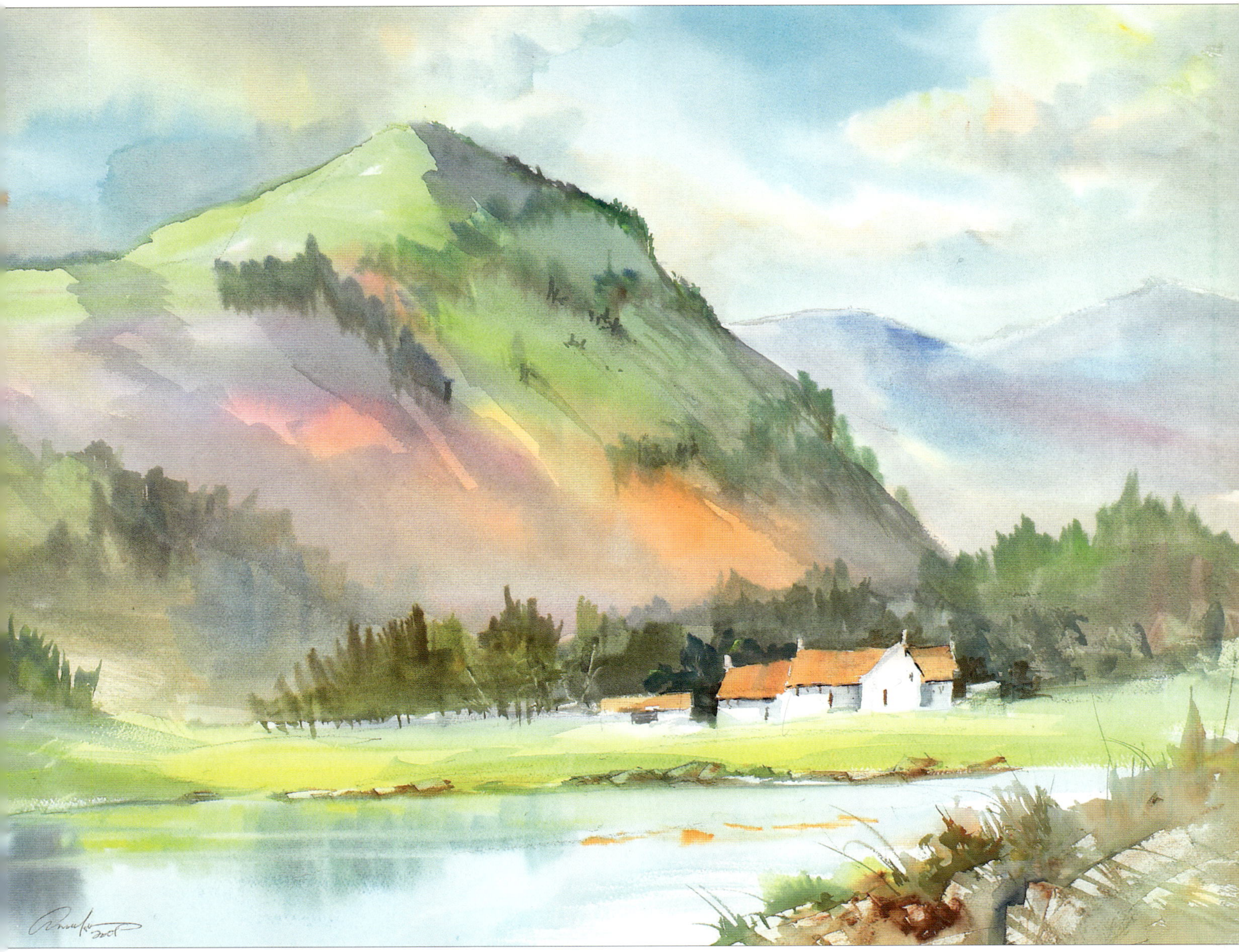

SEARCH PRESS

First published in Great Britain 2009

Search Press Limited
Wellwood, North Farm Road,
Tunbridge Wells, Kent TN2 3DR

ISBN: 978-1-84448-333-4

Suppliers
If you have any difficulty obtaining any of the materials and equipment mentioned in this book, please visit the Search Press website: www.searchpress.com

Publishers' note
All the step-by-step photographs in this book feature the author, Arnold Lowrey, demonstrating his watercolour painting techniques. No models have been used.

Please note that when removing the perforated sheets of tracing paper from the book, score them first, then carefully pull out each sheet.

Printed in China

Page 1

A Green Hill Far Away

76 x 56cm (30 x 22in)

Although the farm buildings are fairly prominent, the hill is the dominant focal point in this painting. I have used complementary colours (red) to the greens to make it come alive.

Opposite

A Burst of Sun

76 x 56cm (30 x 22in)

Sometimes bursts of sunlight appear through patches of cloud, lighting up parts of the countryside. I have tried to capture this effect in this painting. The rock textures were created by scraping out the paint using a safety razor blade.

Dedication

To my wife, Joy, and family, and also to Paul Arnott who helps me enormously.

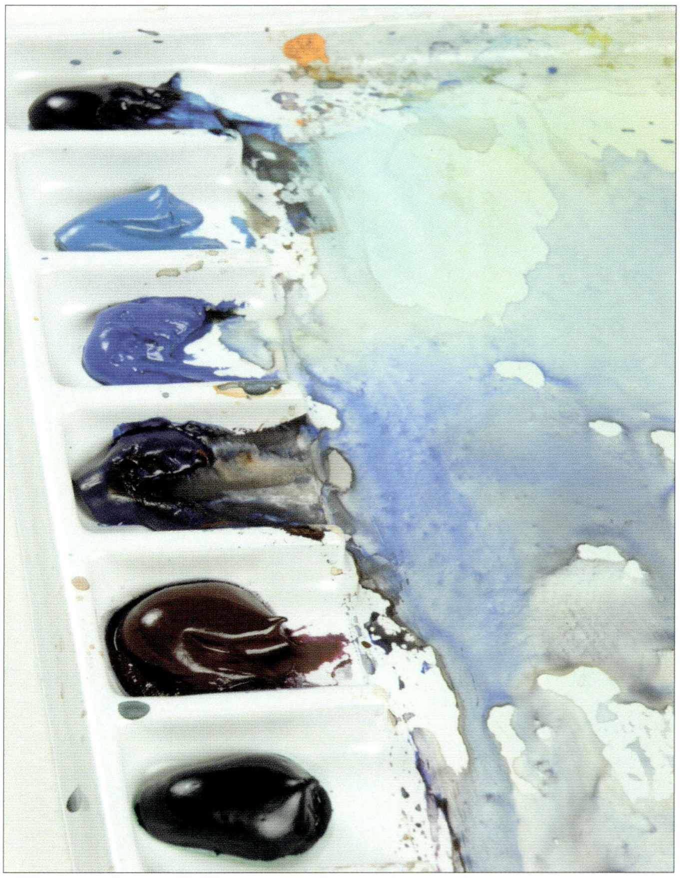

Acknowledgements

I wish to thank Katie Sparkes, my editor, for her invaluable assistance in creating this book, Debbie Patterson for her wonderful photography, and Roz Dace and everyone else at Search Press Ltd. Also my family, friends and all the students who have supported me through the ebbs as well as the flows.

Contents

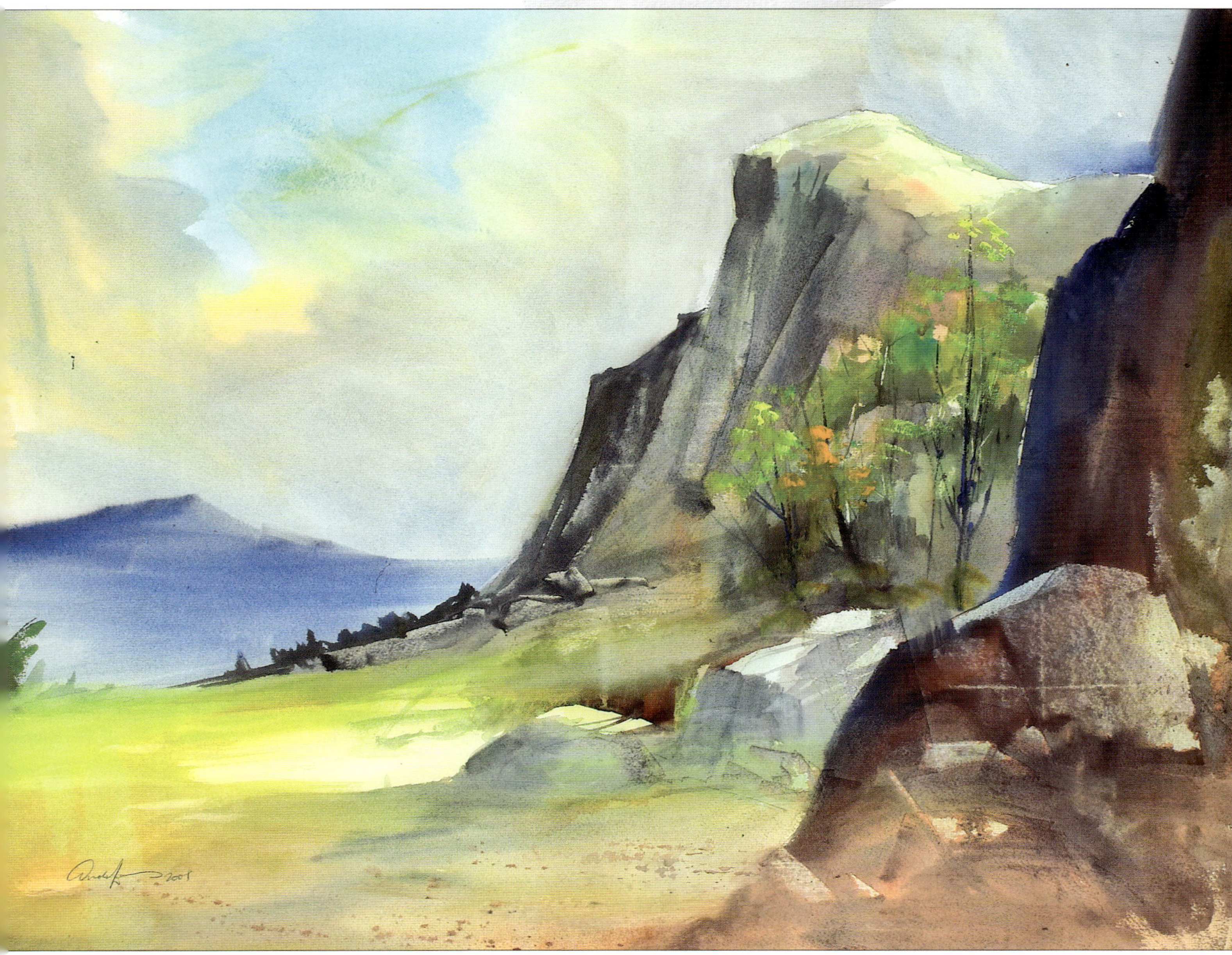

Introduction

I took up art as a hobby thirty-five years ago to act as a foil to my career in engineering. Little did I realise that I had embarked on one of the four great enquiries of life – the other three being science, philosophy and theology. I started attending a local evening class thinking it would be a restful occupation. That was another shock, as painting requires an intense concentration which can be very tiring. However, the stress caused is good stress because it cancels out the bad stresses we have in our daily lives. Remember, the reason we want to paint is not that it is restful but because it is very, very interesting. Unlike a jigsaw puzzle where the more you complete the less there is to do, with painting the more you do, the more you realise there is to learn!

One of the big problems that beginners face is the inability to draw well, which can ruin their attempts to create a good painting. This book therefore includes tracings for each project, and an additional tracing for the picture shown opposite, that can be transferred easily to watercolour paper. This allows you to skip over the drawing stage and concentrate entirely on the painting techniques.

Painting mountains and hills can be exciting and rewarding if approached in the right way. The biggest mistake made by beginners is not to consider the quality of the silhouettes and shapes that make up the picture. Most great paintings are not exact copies of what they represent; more often than not the artists have altered what they see to make them more interesting and attractive to the eye. Remember, good shapes make great paintings.

Your journey into painting will encompass two main disciplines – art and craft. The craft side is, for example, learning about paint handling, colour mixing, how to paint skies and seas, etc.; the art is about how you interpret your feelings for the subject. The five paintings in this book help you practise your craft and, if you wish, a little of the art to help you 'sing with your own voice'.

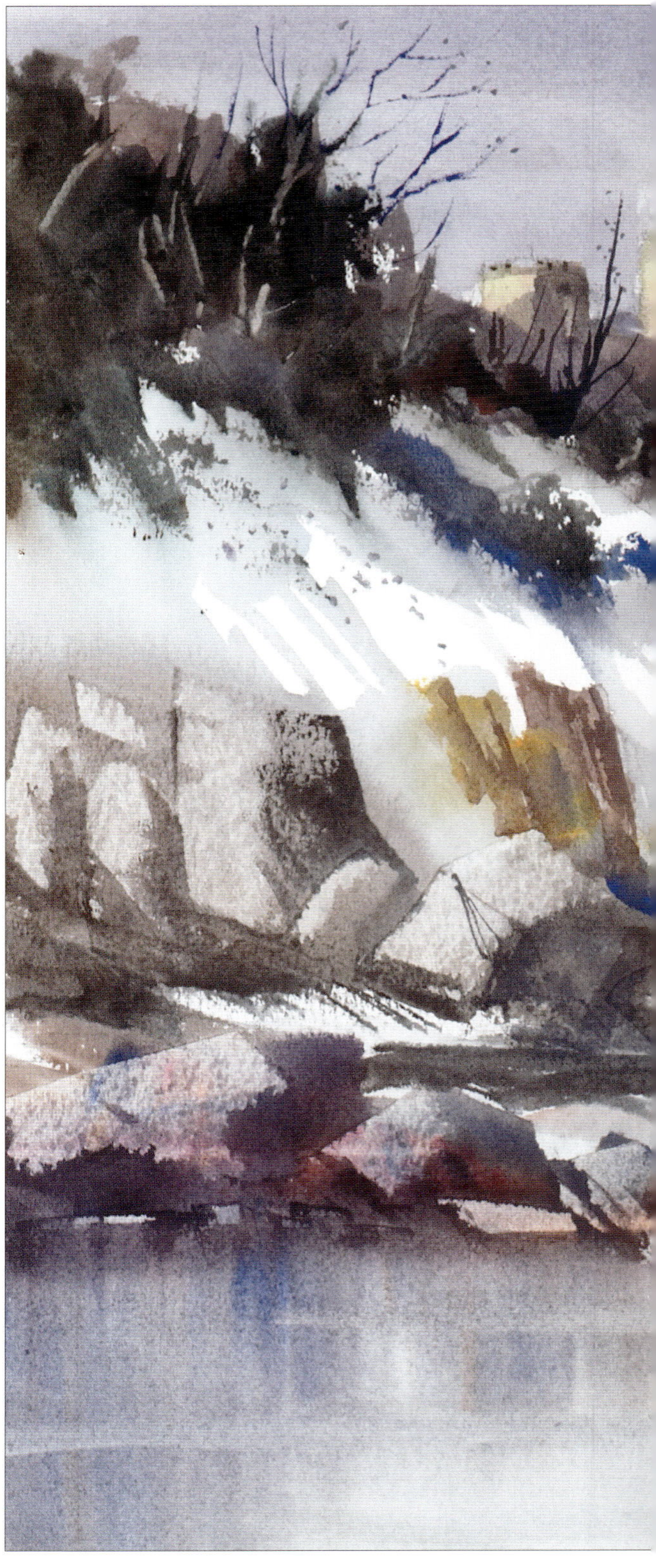

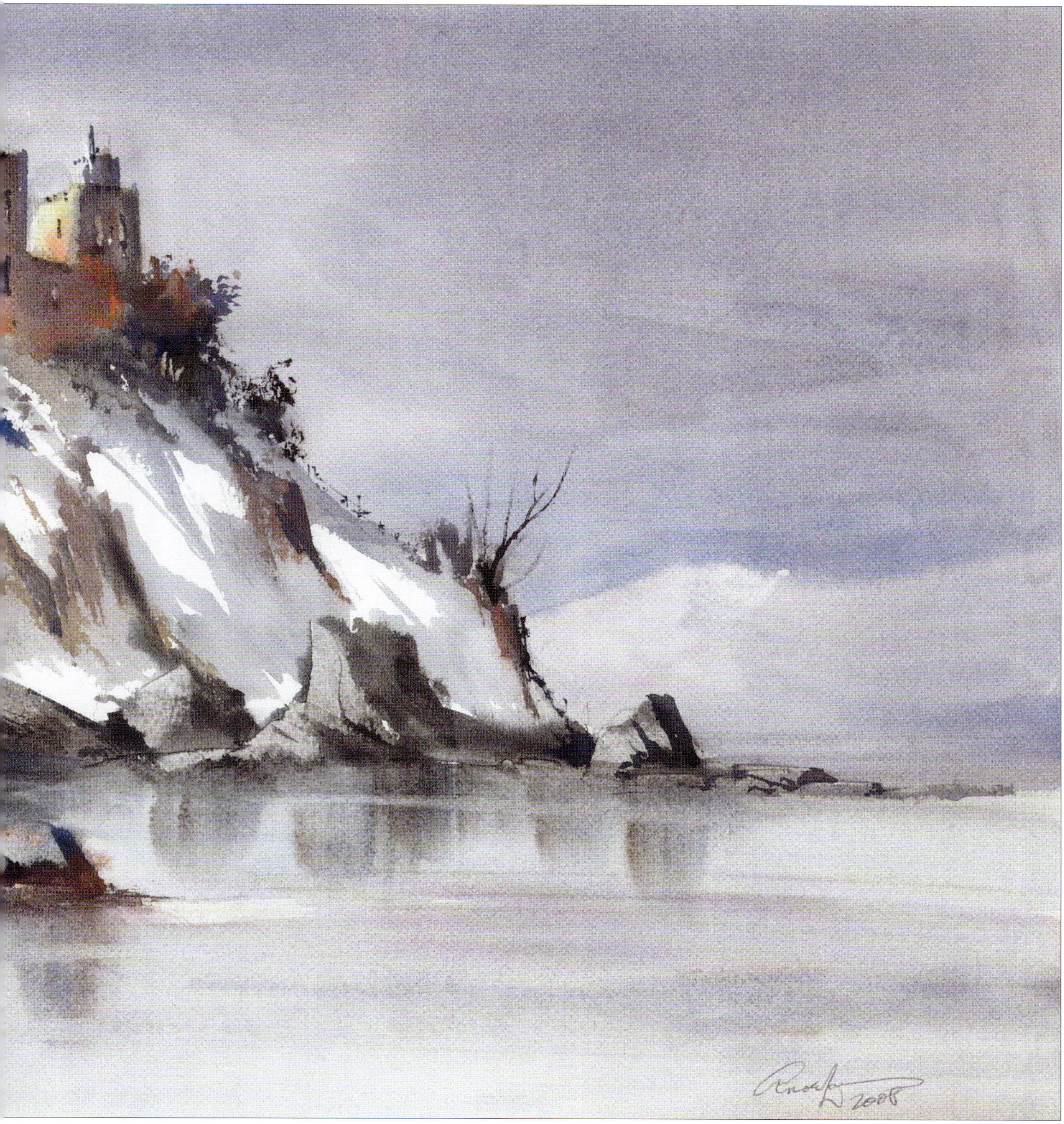

Castle

42 x 29.5cm (16½ x 11½in)

This hillside, with its castle and trees, forms an interesting shape with many textures. The surrounding sky and water are soft to balance it. Some warm colours were placed in the hillside and castle to draw the eye. In general, paintings that include some warm colours are far more appealing than those that do not. The tracing for this painting is available at the front of the book (tracing 1).

Materials

Paints

Watercolour paints are available in artist and student qualities. Student quality paints cost less because they contain cheaper alternatives to some of the more expensive pigments found in artist quality paints. I would recommend starting with student colours and working up to the more expensive ones later.

I always use tubes of paint as opposed to pans. The colours, when used straight from the tube, are more intense, and I find it far easier and quicker to mix accurate washes on my palette. Pans, however, are better if you intend to paint outdoors as they are easier to transport.

I always use the same colours in my palette, and lay them out as shown opposite. By always placing your colours in the same well of your palette, you will soon get to know where each one is located, which makes colour mixing easier. The palette I use has eight open-ended paint containers on either side of a large, slightly angled mixing area. The lid, which helps keep the paints moist when not in use, slots under the palette to catch excess water.

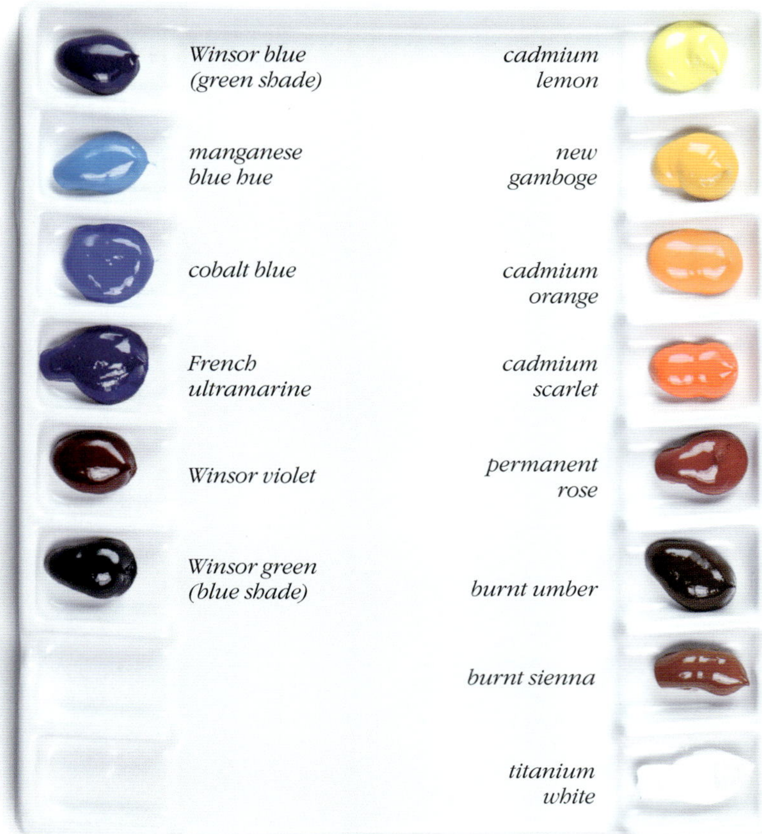

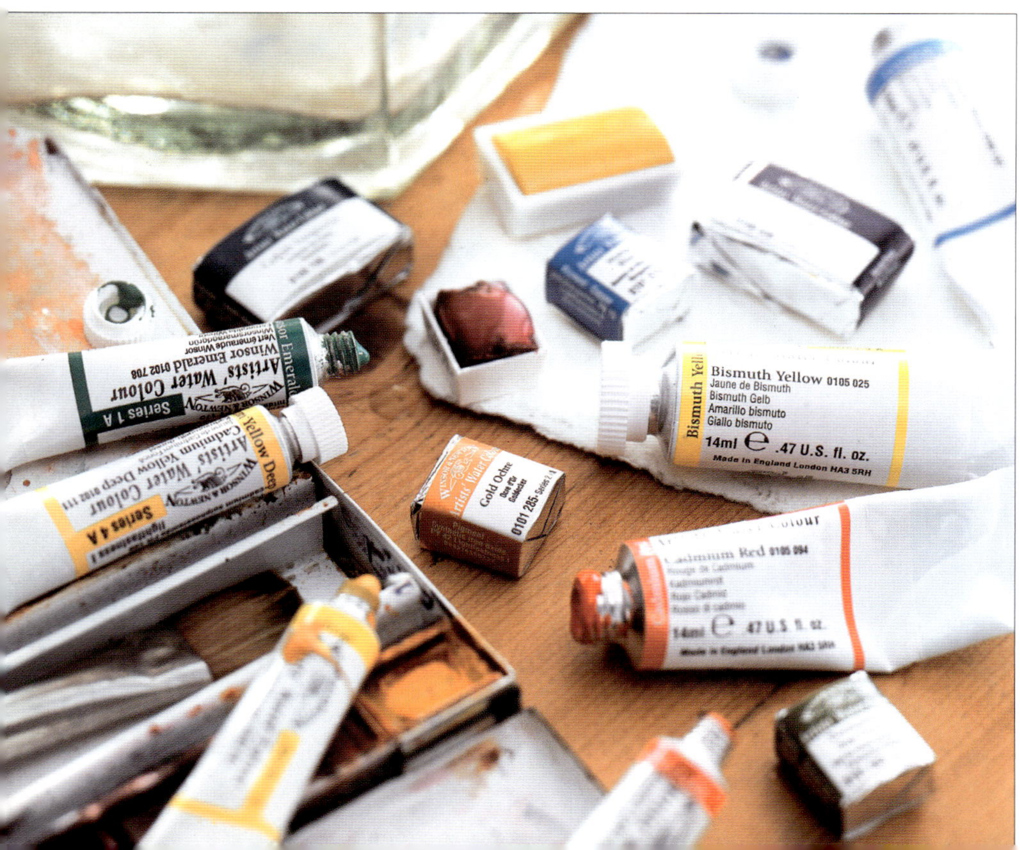

Paints are available in a wide range of colours, and in two forms – tubes or pans.

Paper

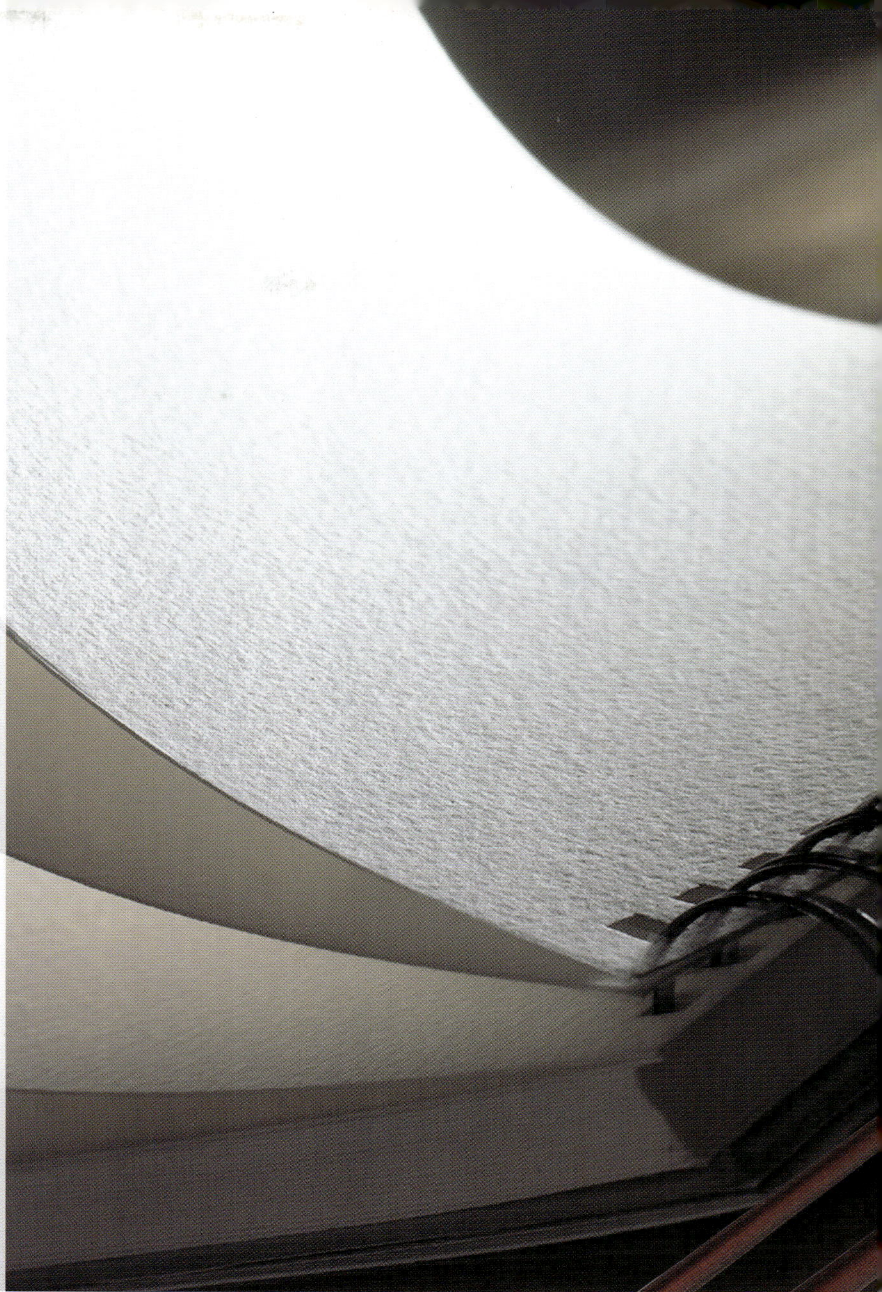

There is a variety of watercolour papers available and you will need to experiment a little to find the one that is right for you. It comes in different textures, from smooth (hot pressed or fine) to rough. NOT paper (cold pressed) has a medium-grade finish and is probably the most suitable for the projects in this book. Thick paper, although more expensive, is less likely to 'cockle' (bend out of shape) when wet; a good weight to use is 300gsm (140lb), but for beginners 180gsm (90lb) would suffice (gsm = grams per square metre). All watercolour papers are sized to help keep the pigments on the paper surface.

Watercolour papers are usually made from wood pulp or cotton (sometimes called rag). Mistakes are easier to sponge out after they have dried on wood-pulp papers, so I would recommend beginners to use these. On cotton papers, however, work that has dried is better protected when you need to paint over it.

Paper comes in pads, blocks or sheets – the way you buy it is entirely up to you. Some artists wet and stretch their papers before starting a painting to ensure it lies flat when finished. However, a beginner can be put off by too much preparatory work; I always simply clip my paper to a board with two bulldog clips and start straight away.

Brushes

There is a huge range of paintbrushes available for watercolour artists, but you only need to buy three or four initially. Sable brushes are the best quality but are quite expensive, whereas synthetics, though cheaper, offer less control over the amount of water they give out. A good compromise are sable-nylon mixes that perform well and are reasonably priced.

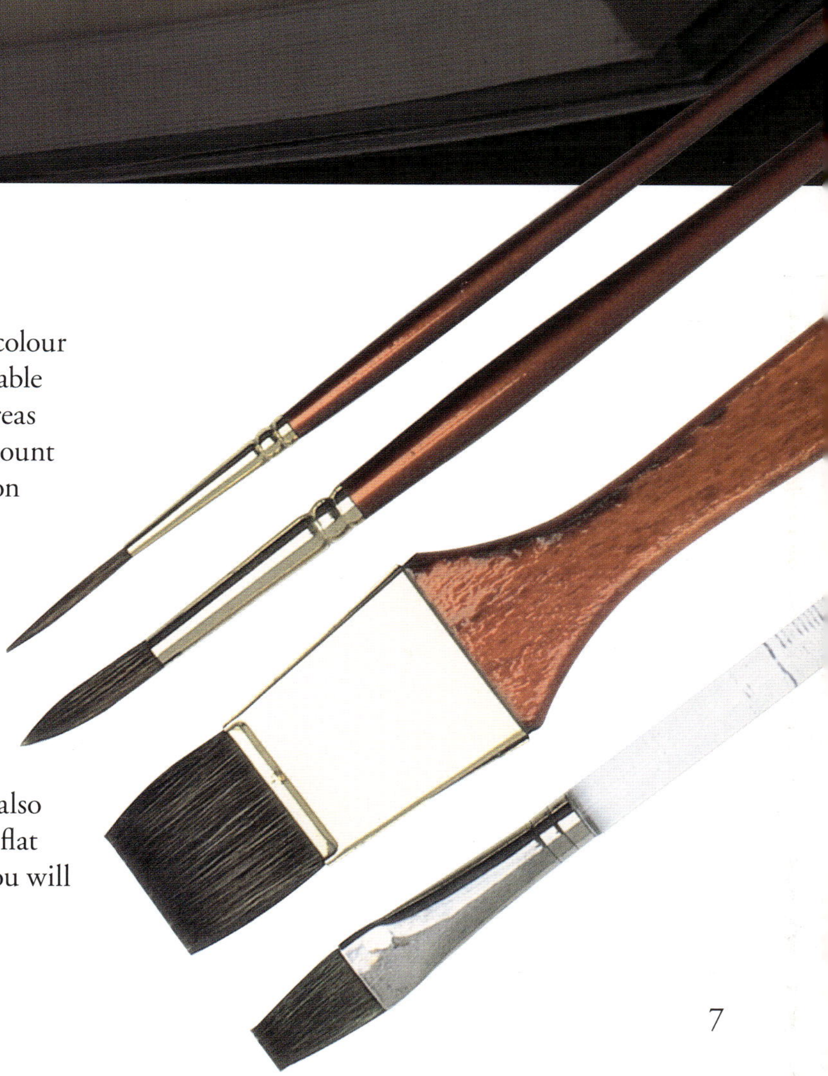

The picture opposite shows the brushes I use. From top to bottom they are: a no. 3 sable-nylon rigger; a no. 8 sable round brush; a 25mm (1in) sable-nylon flat brush (also known as a one-stroke brush); and a 13mm (½in) nylon flat brush with a scraper end. For the projects in this book you will need only the two flat brushes and the no. 3 rigger.

Other materials

I use a soft **4B pencil** for drawing the outline of a composition directly on to watercolour paper and for scribbling over the back of a tracing before transferring the design; a hard **HB pencil** is then used to go over all the lines of the tracing to transfer it to the watercolour paper. A **kneadable putty eraser** is useful for removing unwanted pencil marks – it is extremely soft, absorbs the graphite into itself and does not damage the paper. A **safety razor blade** is extremely useful – use the flat edge of the blade to scrape shapes out of wet paint and the tip for scratching bright highlights out of dry paint. **Kitchen towel** is ideal for lifting out colour, drying brushes and mopping up spills. Small pieces of **sponge** are also useful for lifting out colour. **Masking tape** can be used to attach a sheet of watercolour paper to your work surface. Finally, I use a **water pot** with a ridged base, which is useful for cleaning my brushes between washes, and a **household sponge** for cleaning my palette.

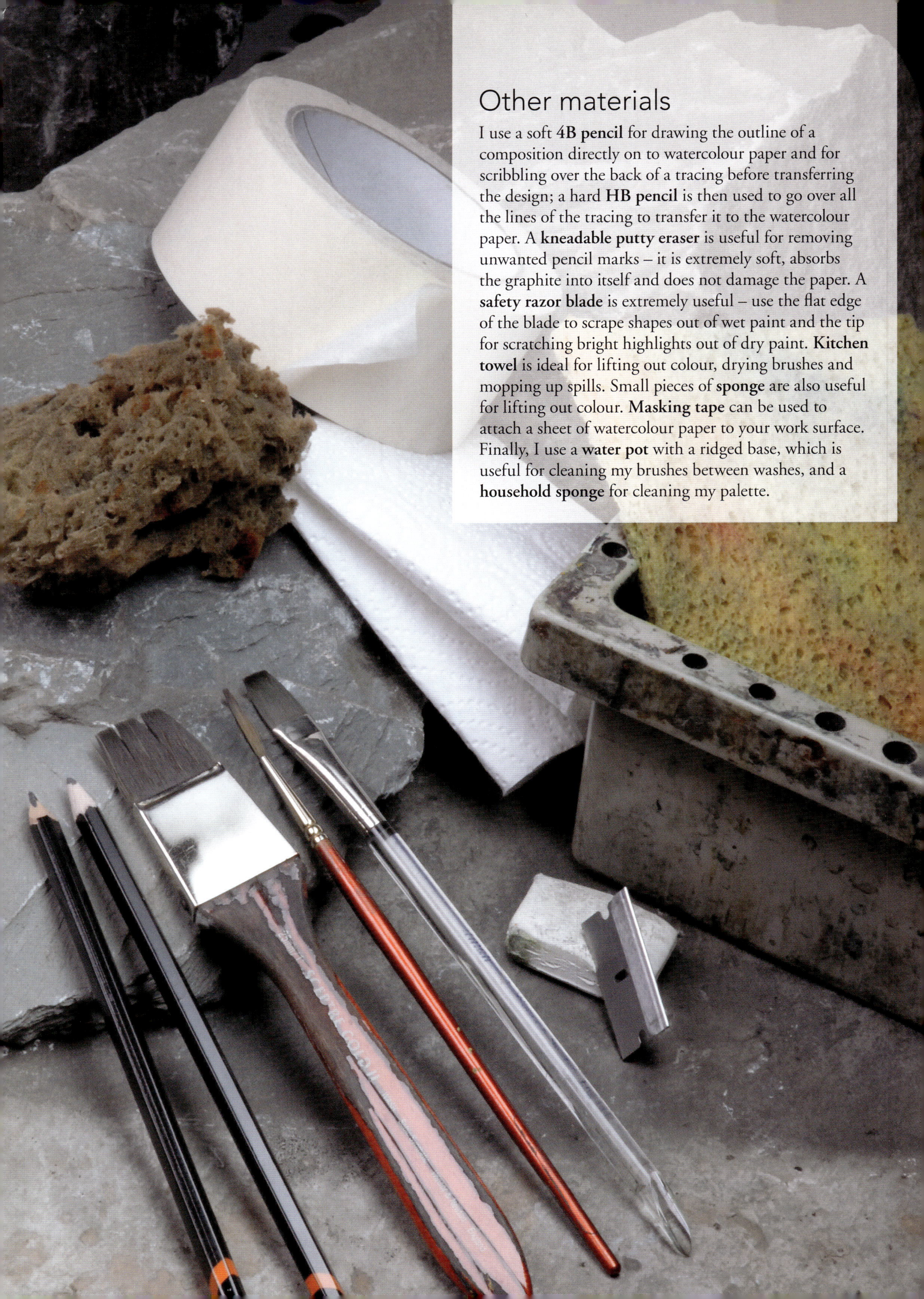

Transferring the image

Transferring the image to your watercolour paper could not be easier. Simply pull out the tracing you want to use from the front of the book (remember to score along the perforated line first) and follow the instructions below. You should be able to reuse each tracing several times, even without going over the pencil lines again.

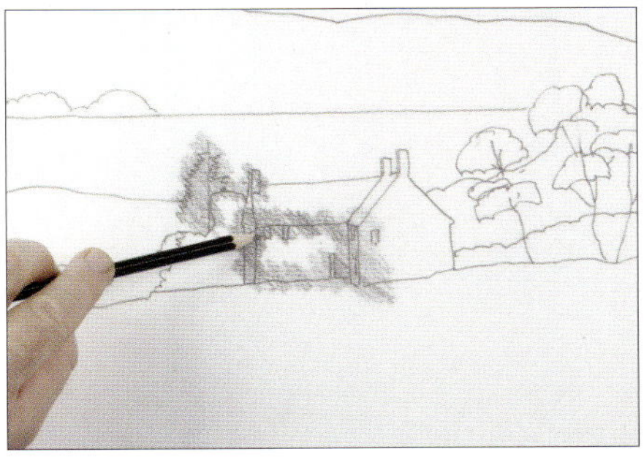

1 Place your tracing face-down on some scrap paper. Go over all the lines on the back using a soft 4B pencil. This is a section from the Distant Hills project on page 10.

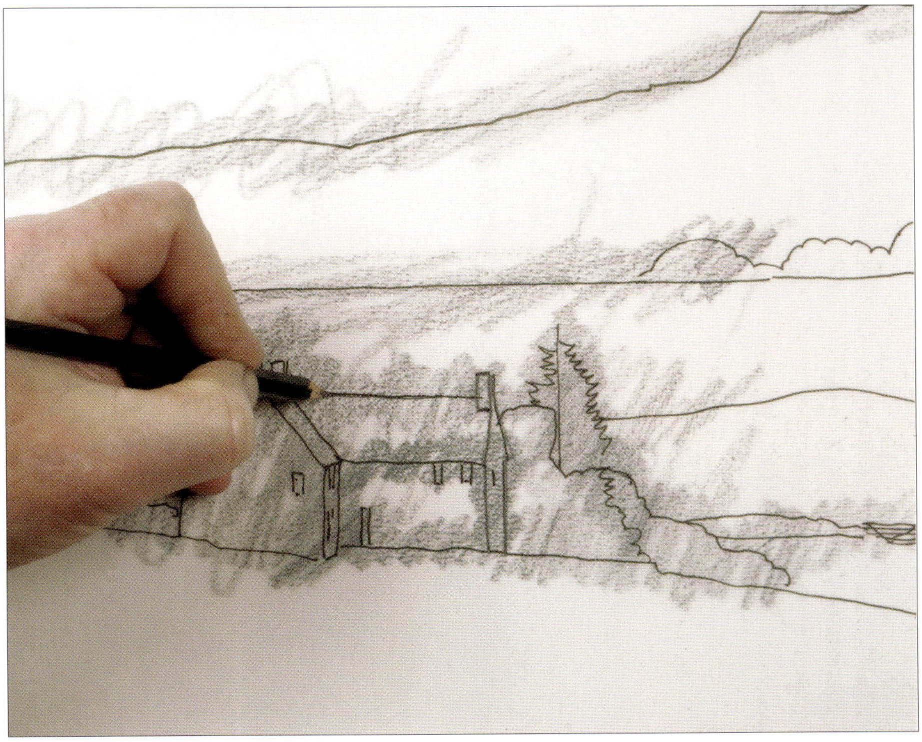

2 Tape a sheet of watercolour paper down on a board using masking tape, and place the tracing, face-up, on top. When you have positioned the tracing accurately, tape down the top of the tracing to secure it. Use a hard HB pencil to go over all the lines.

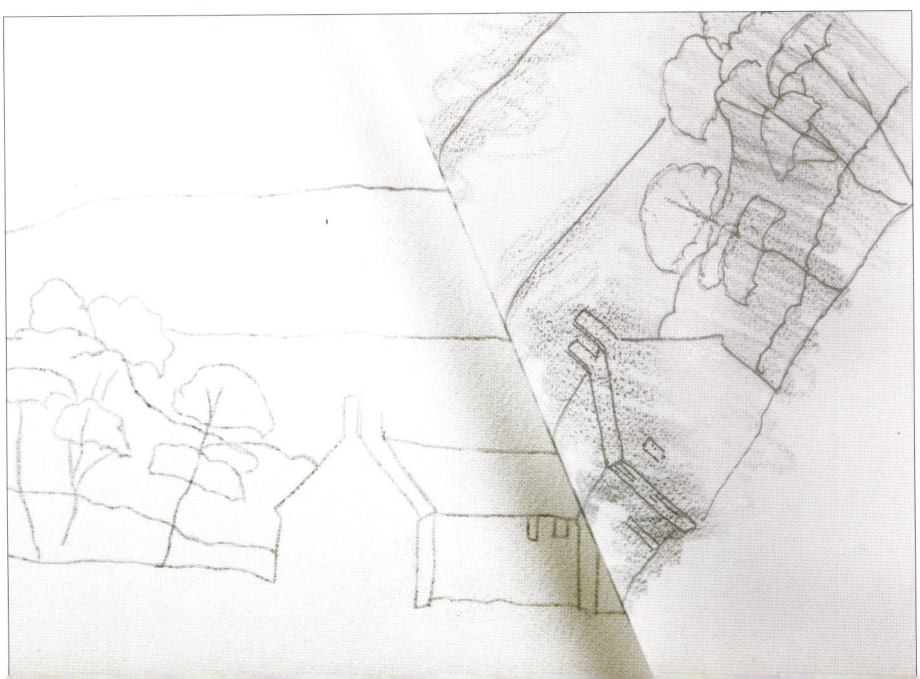

3 Lift up the tracing from the bottom from time to time to check that the image is being transferred properly to the watercolour paper.

Distant Hills

TRACING 2

In this painting I have tried to portray a huge expanse of land with hills in the distance. By placing the house in the foreground I have accentuated the scale of the landscape. The sunlight is coming from the left so I have painted the shadows accordingly, putting some dark trees against the house to make it appear more sunlit.

You will need

180gsm (90lb) NOT watercolour paper
Kneadable (putty) eraser
Safety razor blade
Kitchen paper
Small piece of sponge
Brushes: 25mm (1in) flat brush; 13mm (½in) flat brush with a scraper end; no. 3 rigger
Paints: cadmium scarlet, cobalt blue, French ultramarine, cadmium lemon, new gamboge, Winsor blue (green shade), burnt umber, burnt sienna, permanent rose and titanium white

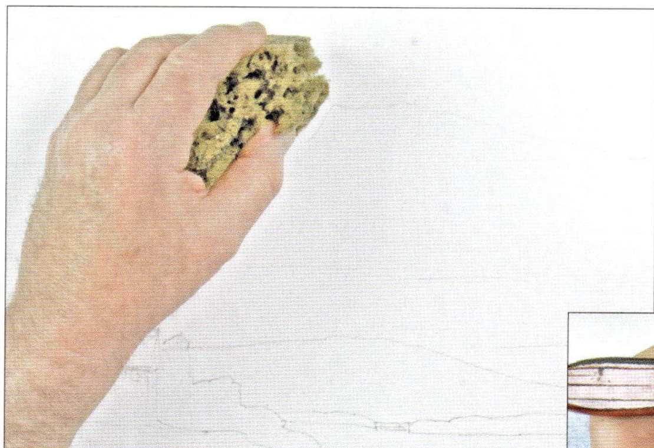

1 Beginning with the sky, dampen the area using a damp sponge. Avoid over-wetting the paper.

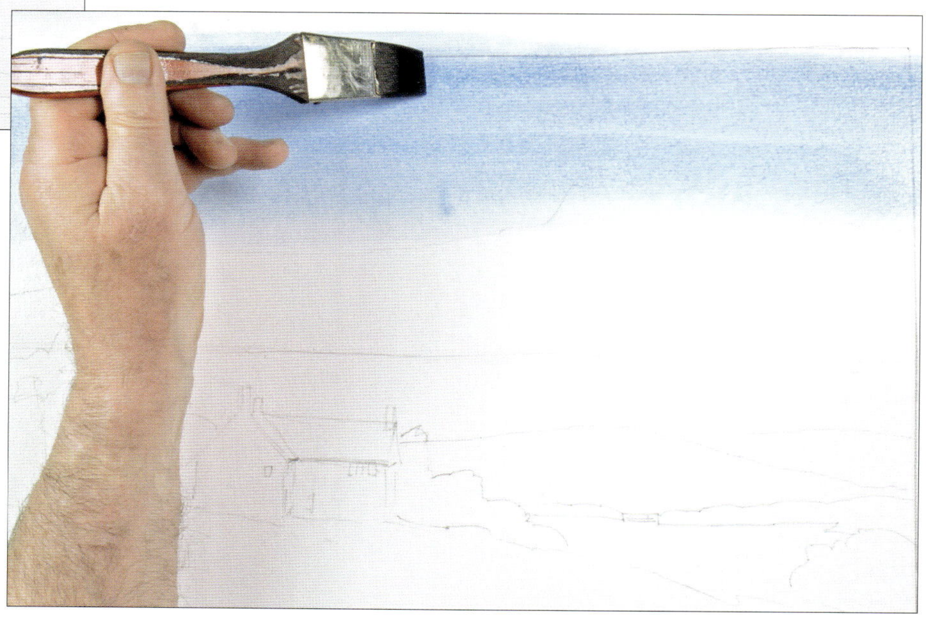

2 Moving on quickly, before the background has time to dry, use the 25mm (1in) flat brush to lay on a wash of cobalt blue. Add some French ultramarine over the top to deepen the colour towards the top of the sky.

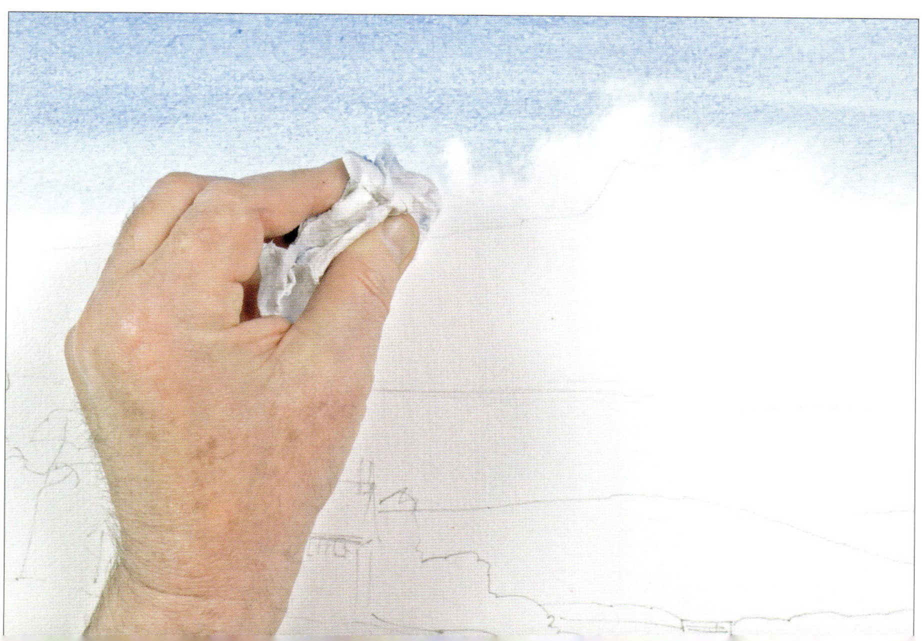

3 Dab out the clouds using a screwed-up piece of kitchen paper. Avoid producing hard edges.

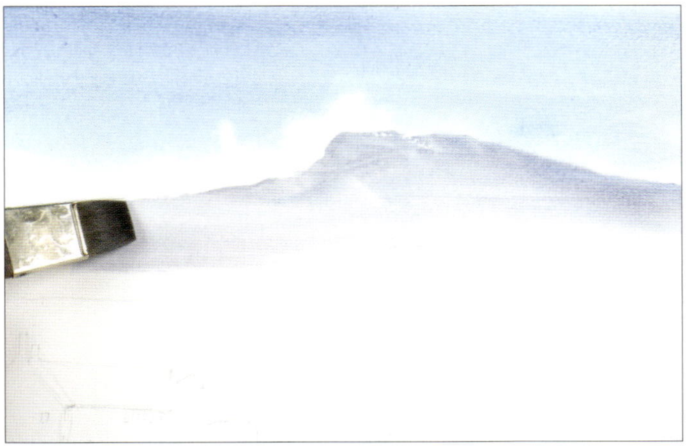

4 For the distant hills, mix some French ultramarine with a touch of cadmium scarlet to create a blue mid-tone and lay in the colour over the peak of the hill, blending it out to a paler tone towards its base.

Tip

Always clean the flat mixing area of your palette with a damp kitchen sponge and wash out your brush before mixing another colour.

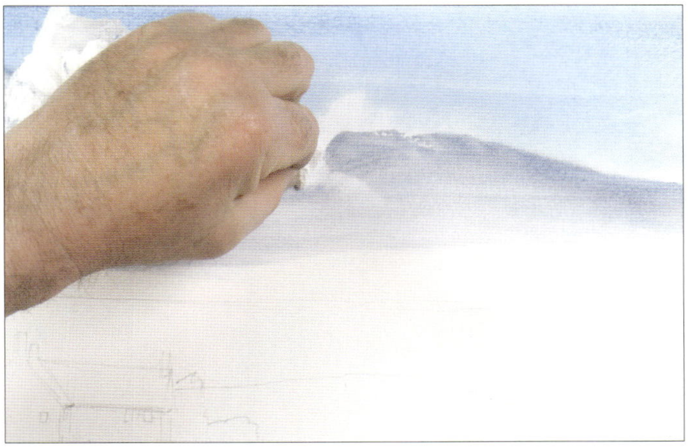

5 Use the kitchen paper to lift out a small cloud near the top of the hill.

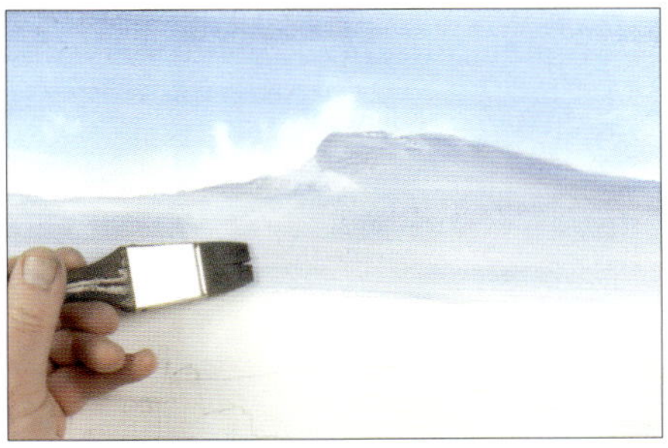

6 Complete the hill using the same colour.

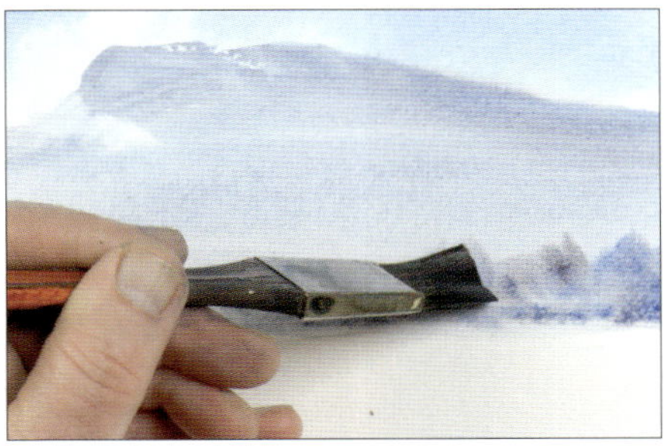

7 Using a stronger version of the same mix, put in the forest at the foot of the hill on the right. Use the side of the brush to paint in the shape of the forest rather than the individual trees.

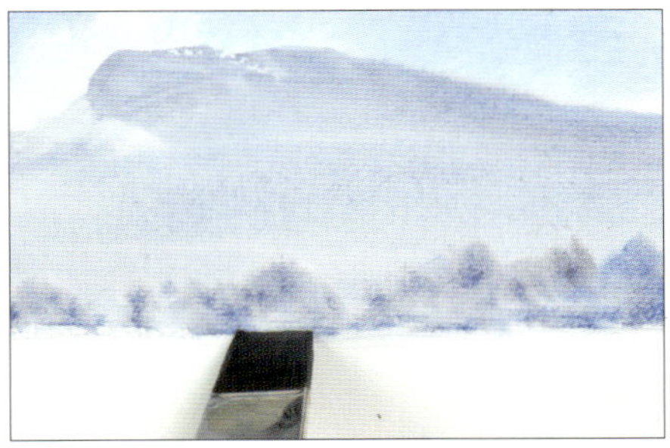

8 Use the flat edge of the brush to even up the bottom of the trees.

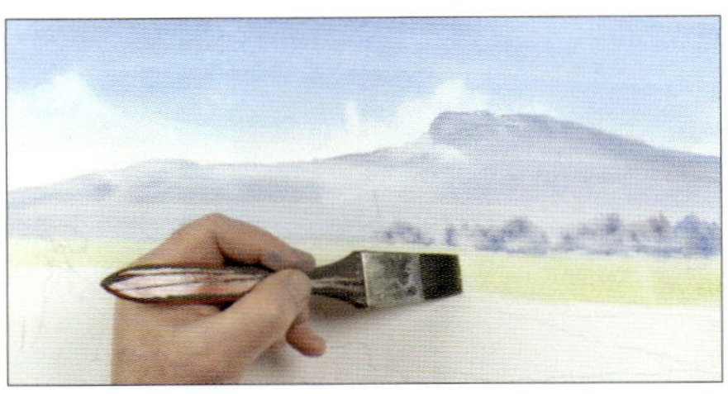

9 Make a mix of cadmium lemon and a hint of cobalt blue, and lay an even wash across the mid-ground.

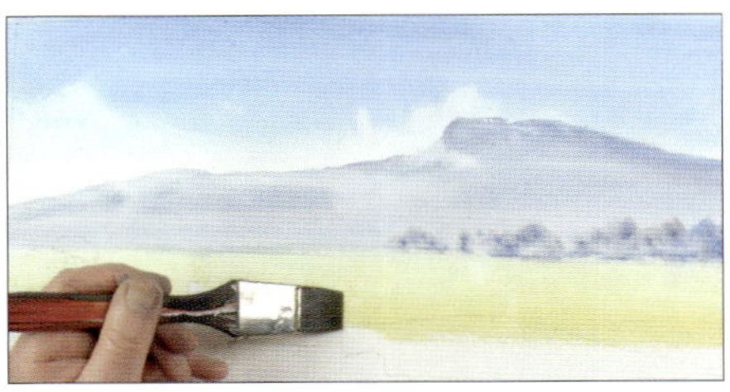

10 Further down the painting, add in some new gamboge to warm up the mix. The transition from cool to warm colours will help bring the picture forwards.

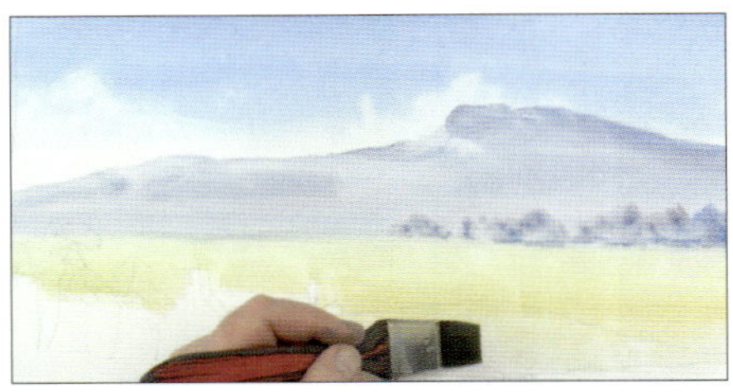

11 Use a damp, clean brush to soften the edge of the paint.

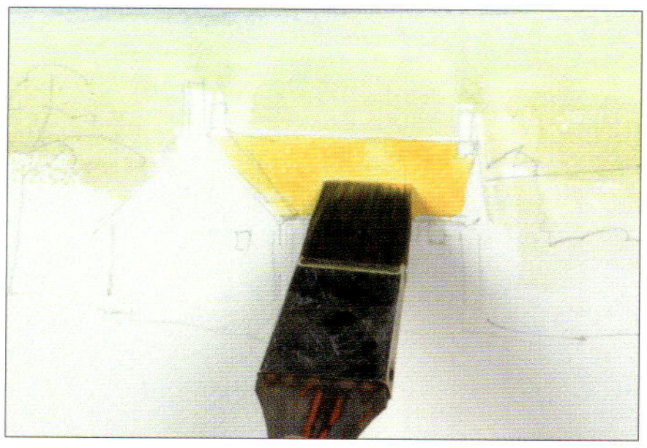

12 Paint the roof of the house using new gamboge applied with the flat edge of the brush.

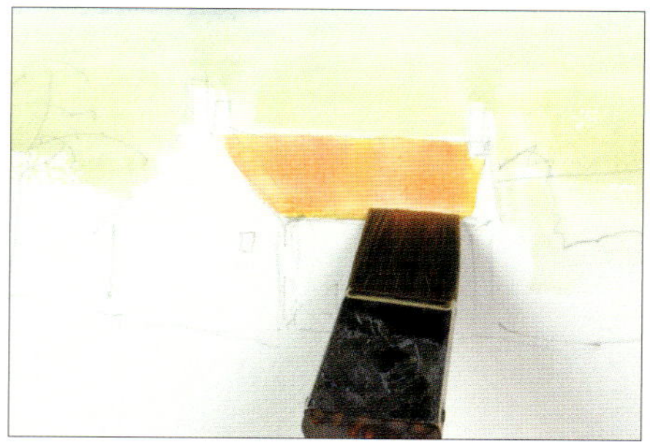

13 Wring out the brush and pick up some cadmium scarlet. Add a little of the colour to the roof, allowing it to blend with the new gamboge.

Tip

To control the amount of water in your brush (and to make sure there is not too much), mix your paint to the right colour with some water on the palette, clean and wring out your brush and then pick up the paint using a single stroke.

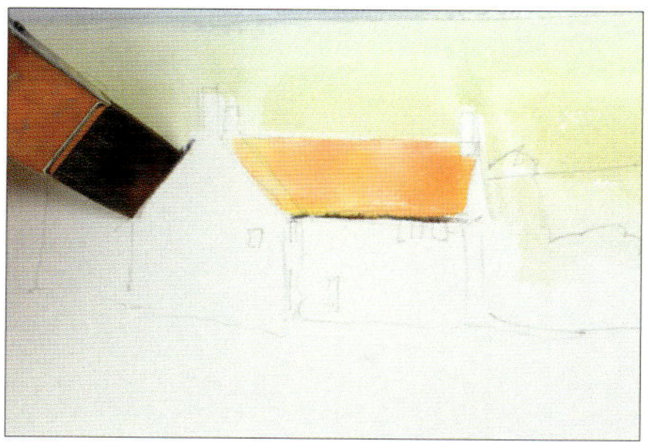

14 Using French ultramarine mixed with a little cadmium scarlet and very little water, dab on the gutters using the flat edge of the brush.

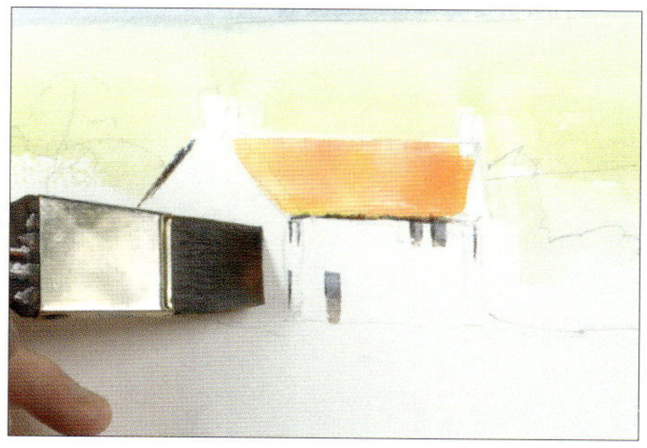

15 For the windows and doors, use the corner of the brush.

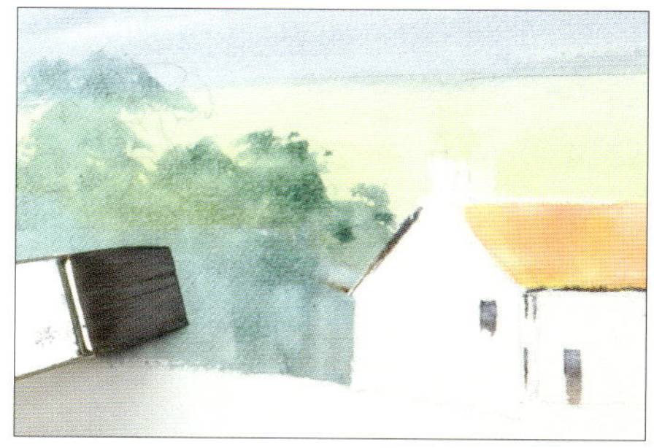

16 While the paint is drying, add the trees surrounding the house. Make a dark green using Winsor blue (green shade) and burnt umber and pick up with a single stroke. Dab on the paint using the side of the brush.

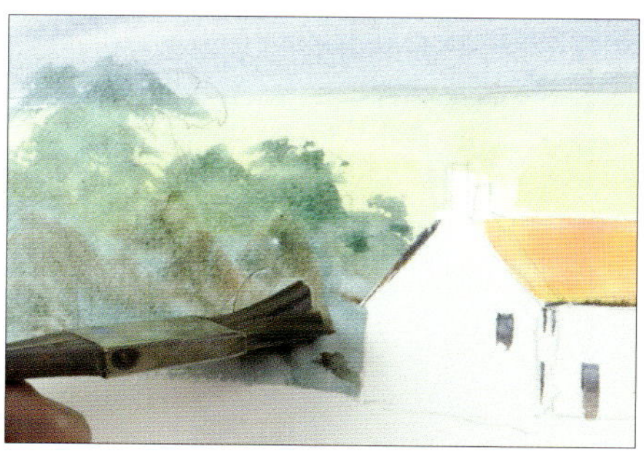

17 Add some warmth to the trees by adding some burnt sienna.

Tip

Dabbing paint on using the side of the brush results in a varied, 'sparkly' finish rather than a flat area of colour.

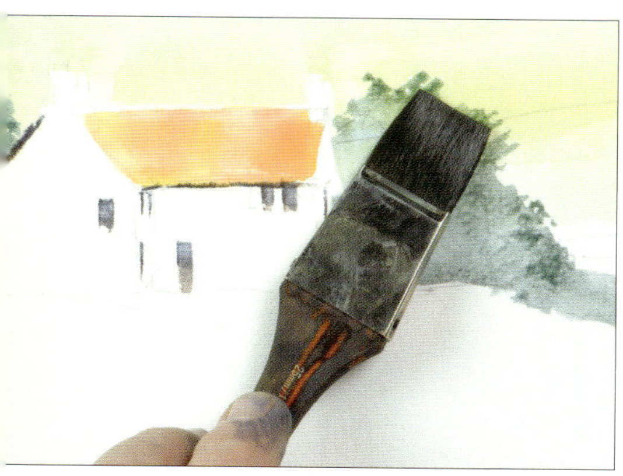

18 Paint the trees on the right-hand side of the house in the same way.

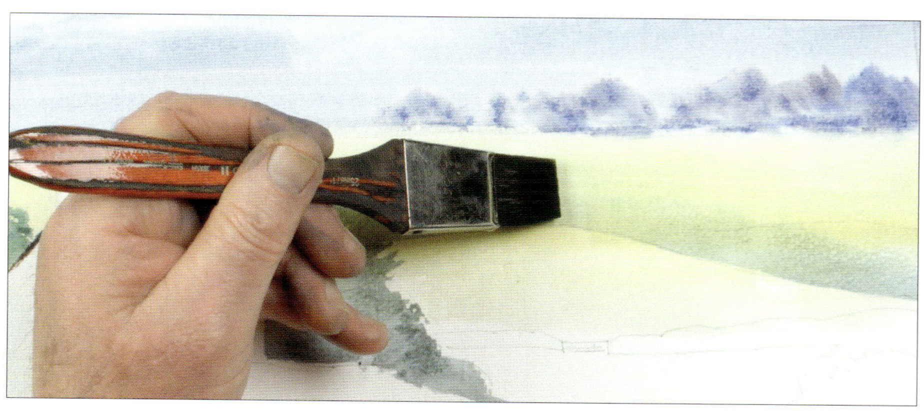

19 Mix some cobalt blue into a little of the green you have just used, and lay a green wash over the mid-ground behind the house. Lose the top edge by blending it in with a clean, damp brush.

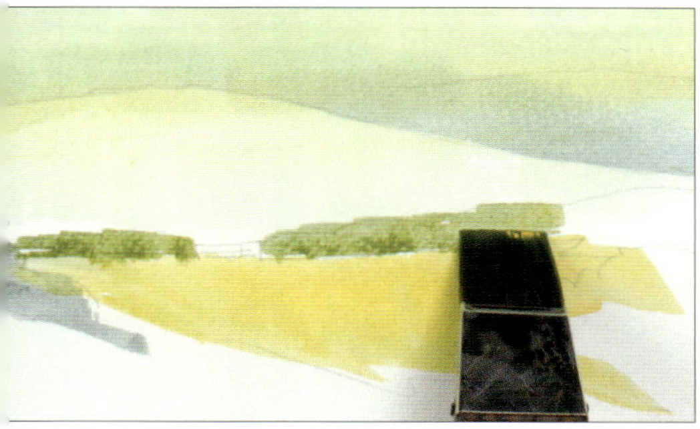

20 Paint in the yellow field just to the right of the house using a wash of new gamboge. Put in the hedgerow at the back of the field using a little new gamboge mixed with French ultramarine.

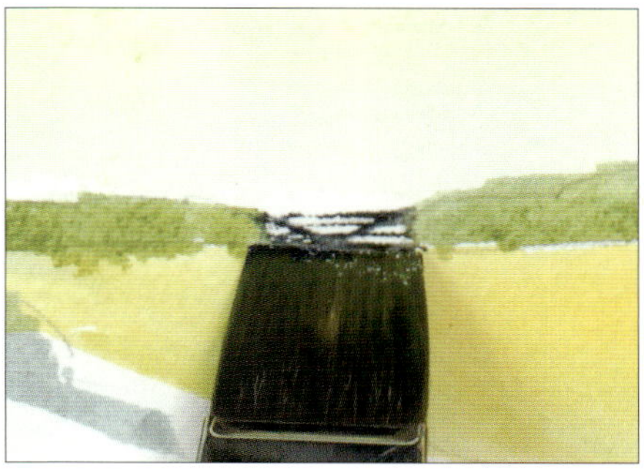

21 Add some more French ultramarine and some burnt umber to the mix, and draw in the gate using the flat edge of the brush.

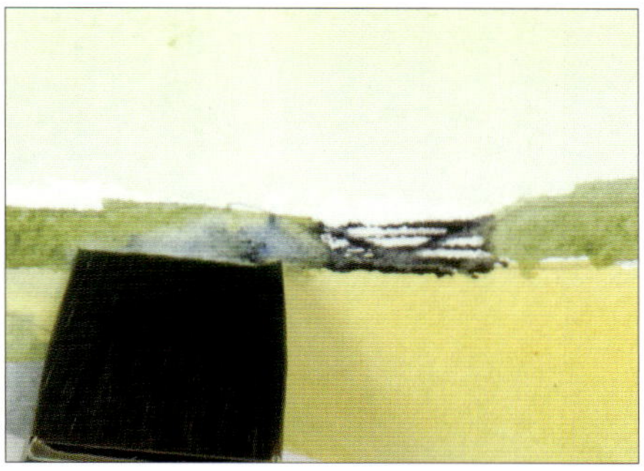

22 Place some darker tones along the base of the hedge.

Tip

Dabbing on a line using the flat edge of the brush creates a more interesting line than one that is simply drawn on.

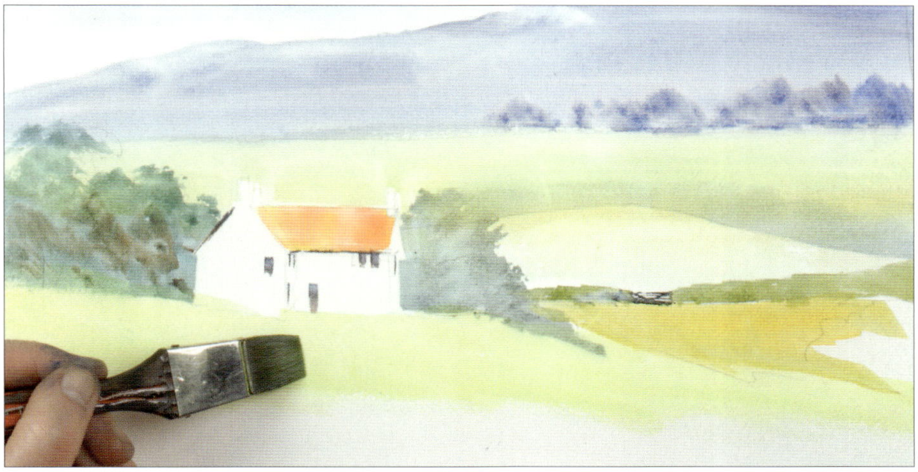

23 Lay a wash of cadmium lemon over the foreground field. Start at the edge of the field nearest the house, and gradually bring the colour forwards.

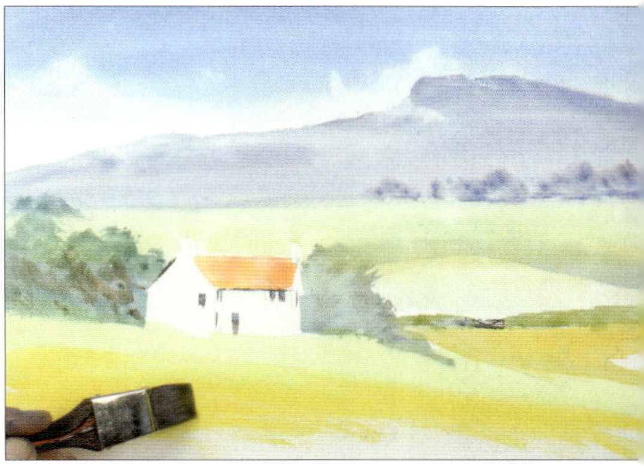

24 As you approach the foreground, introduce some new gamboge into the mix to warm it up.

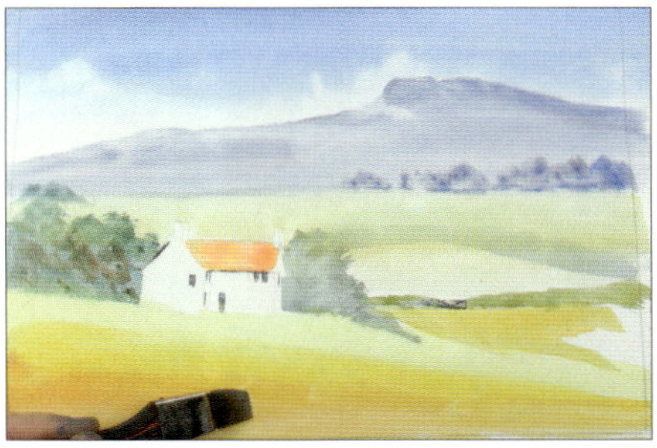

25 Finally, at the front of the picture, introduce some burnt sienna. This creates a gradual transition from cool to warm as you approach the foreground.

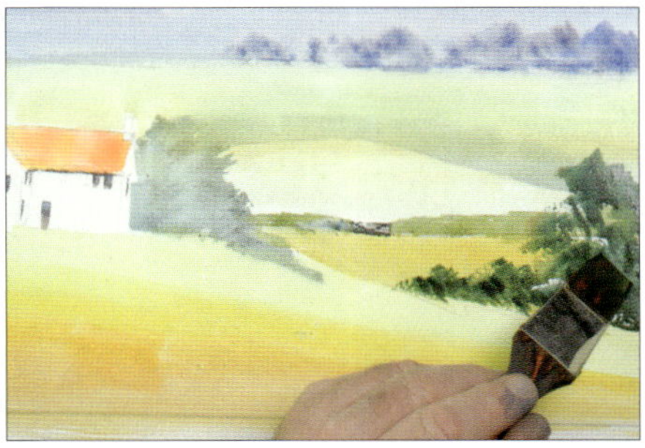

26 Make another dark green mix of Winsor blue (green shade) and burnt umber, and paint in the trees on the far right. Use the side of the brush, as in step 16.

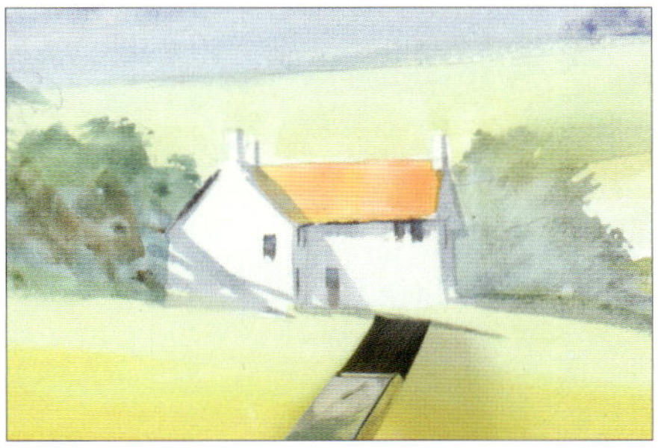

27 Make a mix for the shadows (see the tip box opposite). Paint these on the front and sides of the house, and on the ground just in front of it (the light is coming from the left).

Tip

Shadows in these demonstrations are grey-blue. To produce this colour add to some cobalt blue a tinge of permanent rose (to slightly purple it) and then a tinge of cadmium scarlet (to grey it).

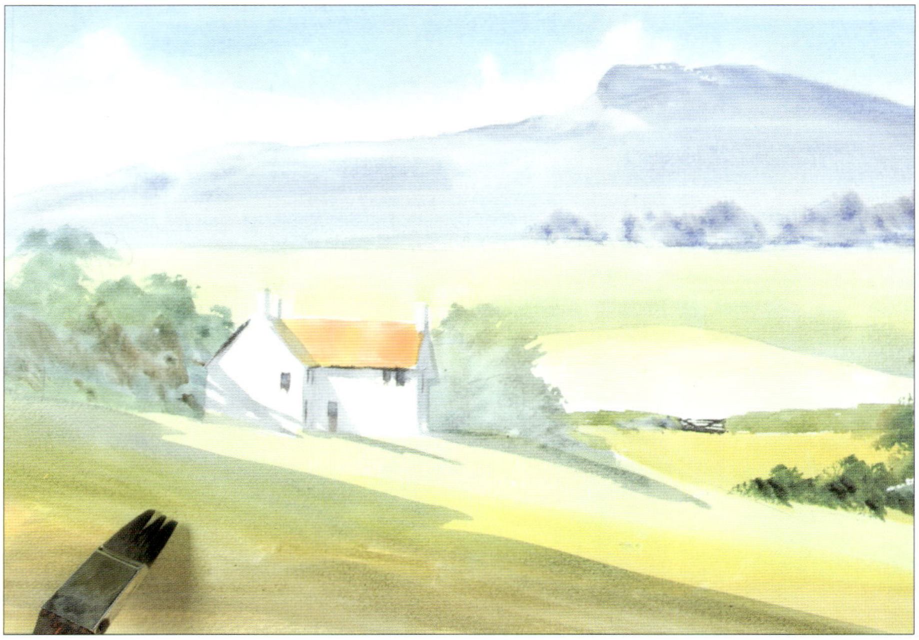

28 Use the same mix to put in the shadows cast by the trees, lying diagonally across the field.

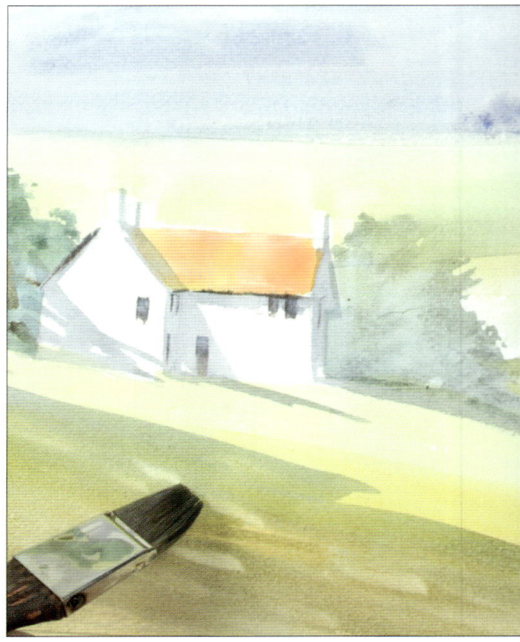

29 Use a clean, damp brush to lift out the dapples of light falling on the ground while the paint is still wet.

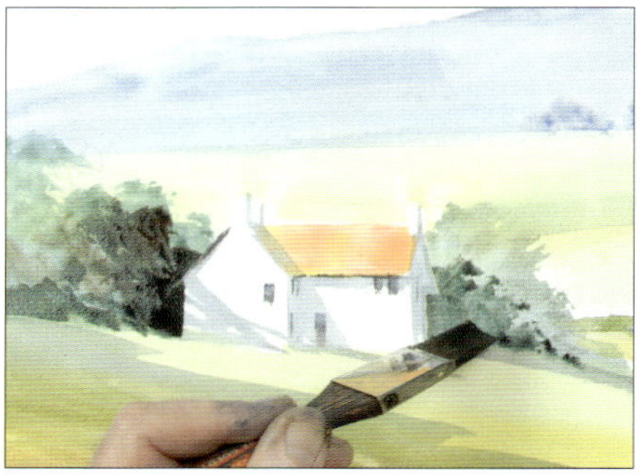

30 To lighten the house, make the trees on either side darker by applying a mix of burnt umber, burnt sienna and Winsor blue (green shade).

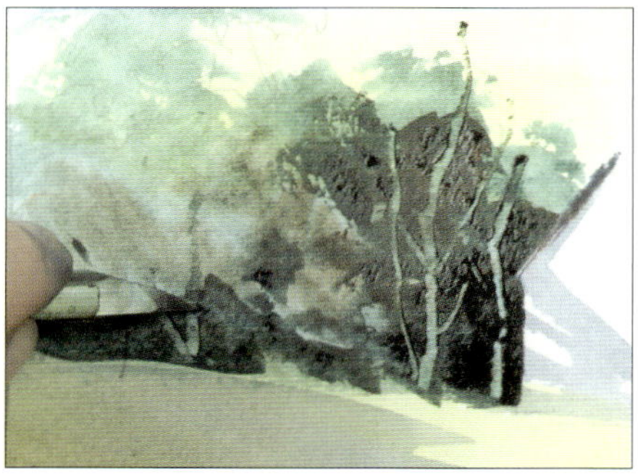

31 While the paint is still wet, use the scraper end of the 13mm (½in) flat brush to scrape out the shapes of some tree trunks and branches on the left.

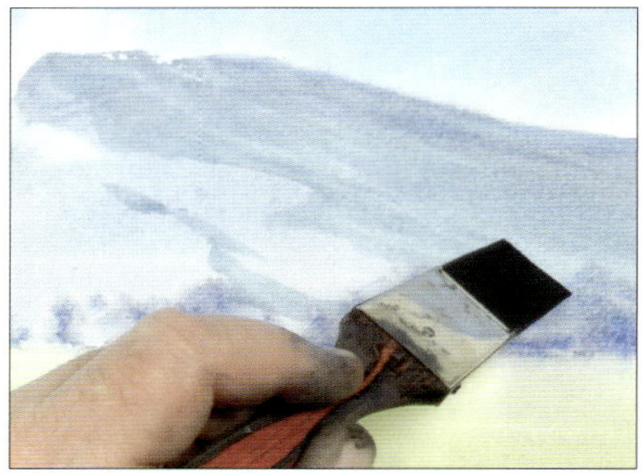

32 Using the shadow mix, place more shadow on the right-facing slopes of the hillside.

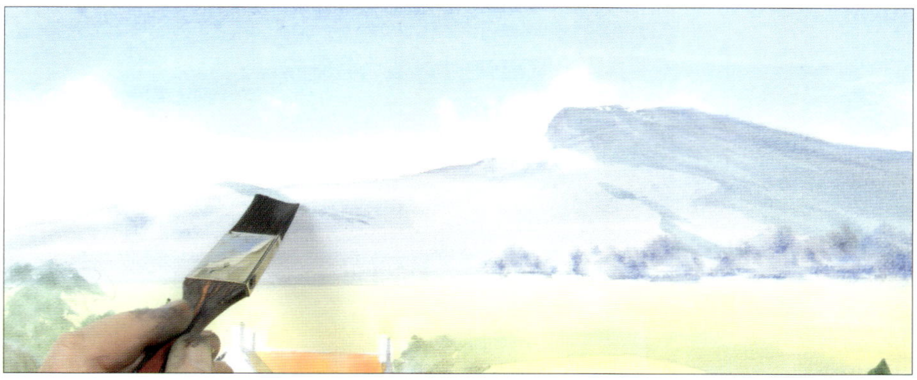

33 Also place some shadows on the top of the hill, on the left. Soften them in with a clean, damp brush.

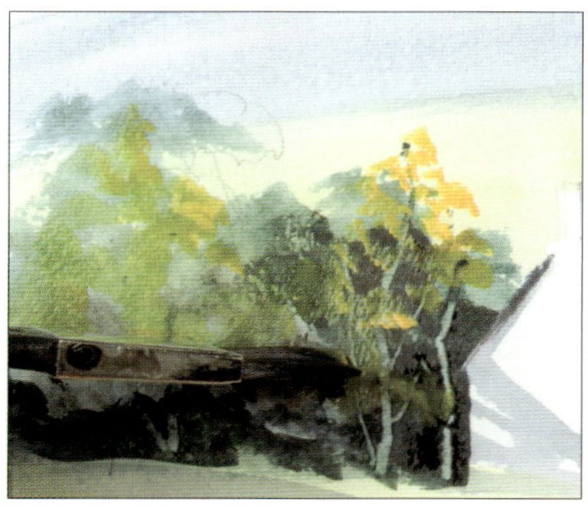

34 Using neat new gamboge, dab in the yellow foliage on the left-hand trees (by now, the paint underneath should be dry).

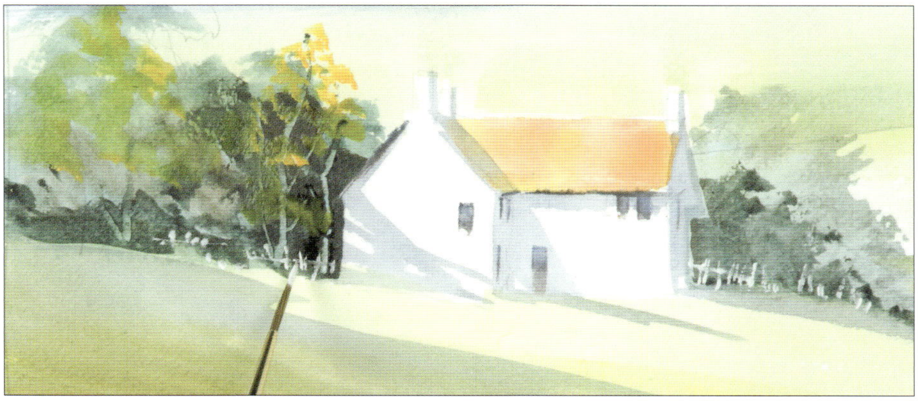

35 Paint in the fence posts either side of the house using titanium white and a no. 3 rigger. Place the posts irregularly and at different angles for a more realistic effect.

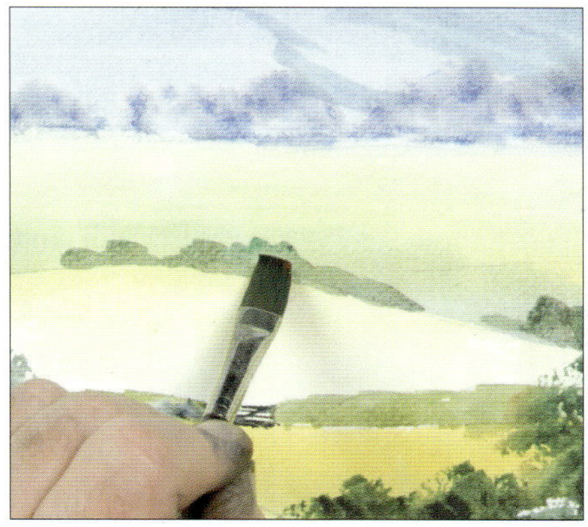

36 Using the 13mm (½in) flat brush, add a little burnt sienna to the dark green mix used in steps 16 and 26, and put in a hedgerow in the mid-ground. Soften the hard edges with a clean, damp brush.

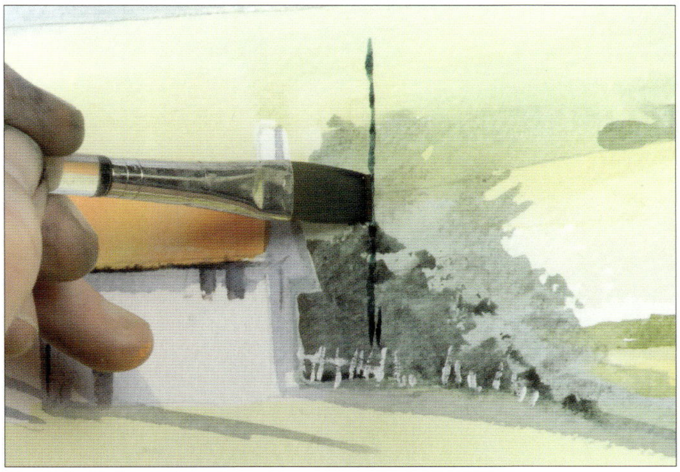

37 Using the same dark green mix, draw in the fir tree to the right of the house.

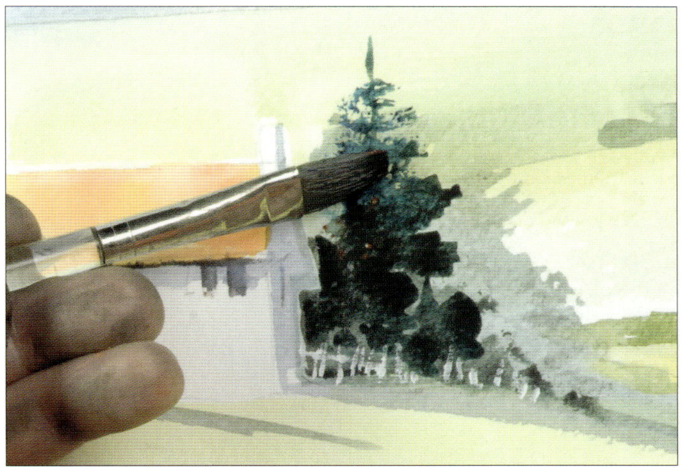

38 Warm up the colour with a little burnt sienna, and paint in the rest of the tree.

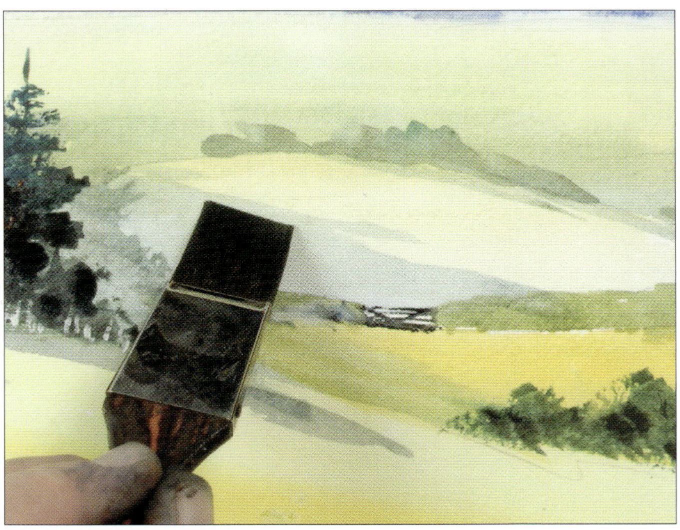

39 Returning to the 25mm (1in) flat brush, strengthen the small field in the middle of the picture by placing a shadow across it.

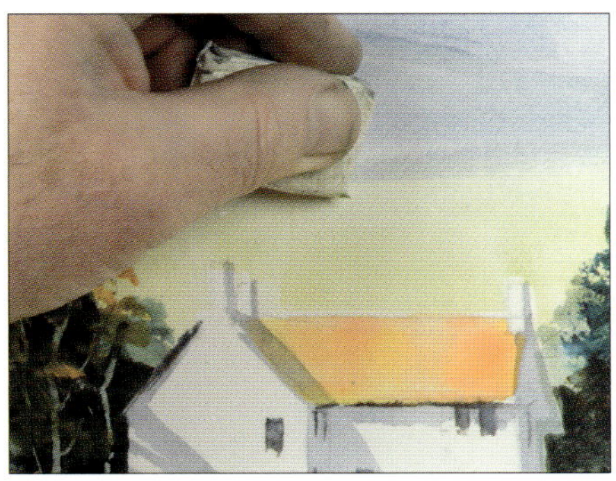

40 When the painting is completely dry, remove any visible lines using a putty eraser.

Overleaf

The finished painting.

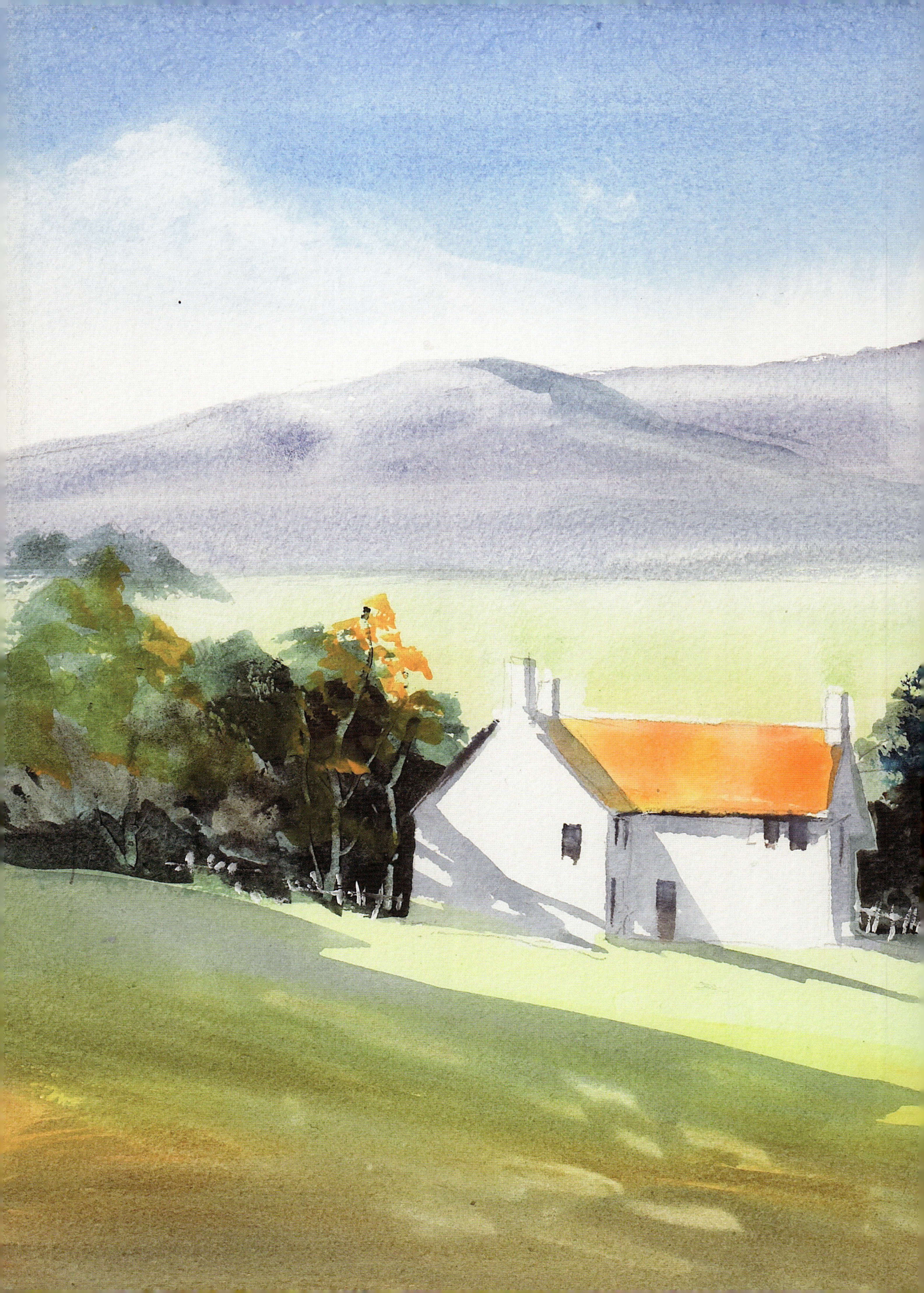

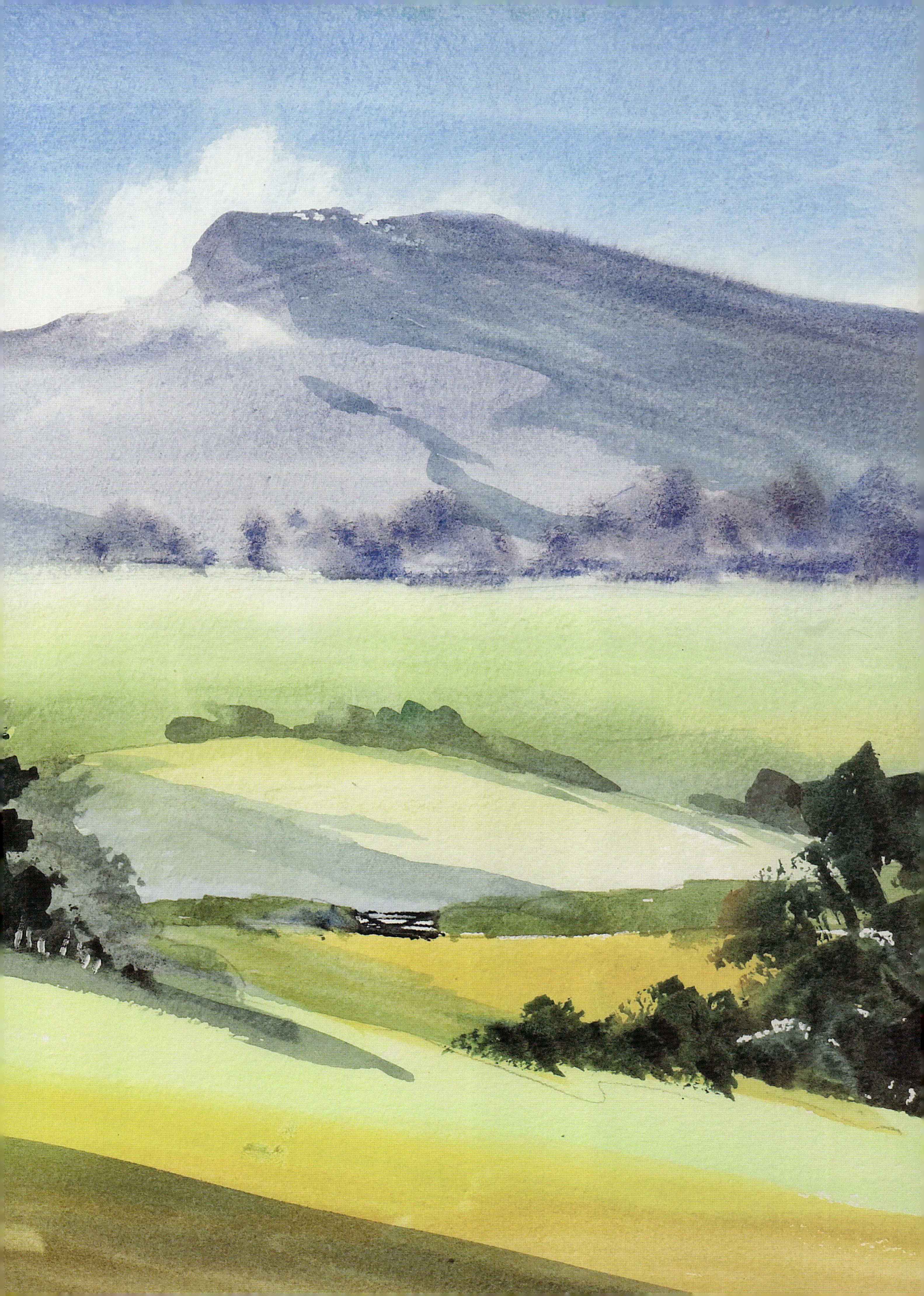

Alpine Scene

TRACING
3

The main elements of this painting are the snow, sky, rocks, trees and shadows. Only the last four are painted – the sunlit snow is unpainted paper. It is important to paint the sky area dark enough so that the white snow contrasts against it. Treat each area of trees as a silhouette and don't attempt to paint every tree! Your aim is to achieve the impression of a forest, rather than a realistic picture of one.

You will need

180gsm (90lb) NOT watercolour paper

Kneadable (putty) eraser

Safety razor blade

Kitchen paper

Small piece of sponge

Brushes: 25mm (1in) flat brush; 13mm (½in) flat brush with a scraper end; no. 3 rigger

Paints: cadmium scarlet, cobalt blue, French ultramarine, new gamboge, Winsor blue (green shade), permanent rose, burnt umber and burnt sienna

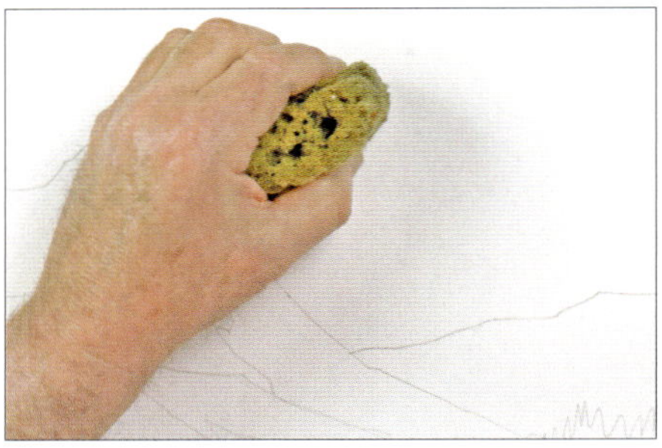

1 Begin, as in the previous project, by dampening the sky area using a damp sponge.

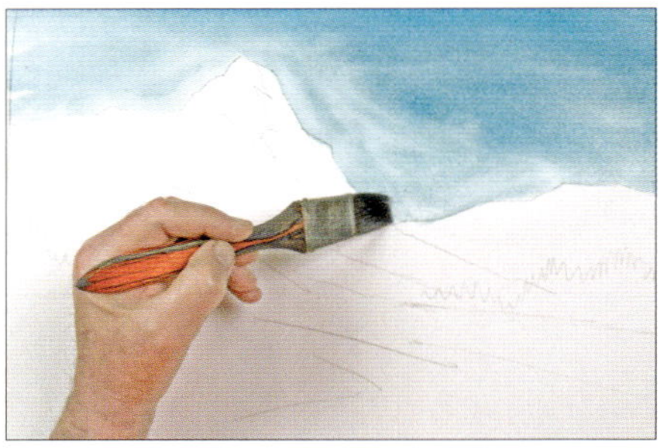

2 While the background is still wet, make a watery mix of Winsor blue (green shade) and a little cadmium scarlet, and brush on the colour using the 25mm (1in) flat brush. Apply the brushstrokes in different directions to eliminate any streaks.

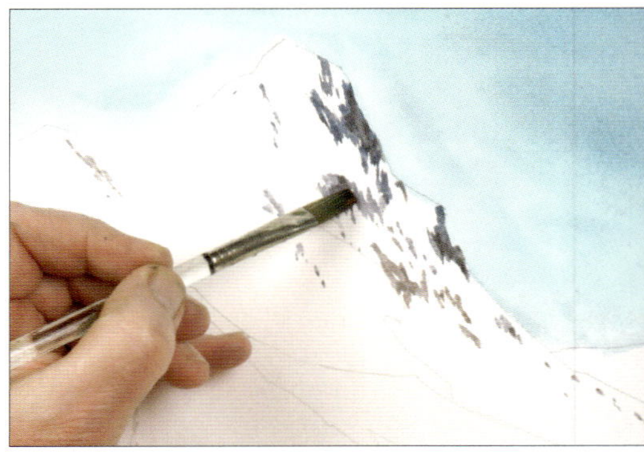

3 Make a grey-blue mix of burnt sienna and French ultramarine, change to the smaller flat brush and put in some of the rocks at the top of the mountain. Apply the paint using the corner of the brush. Add a little more burnt sienna to the mix to vary the colour.

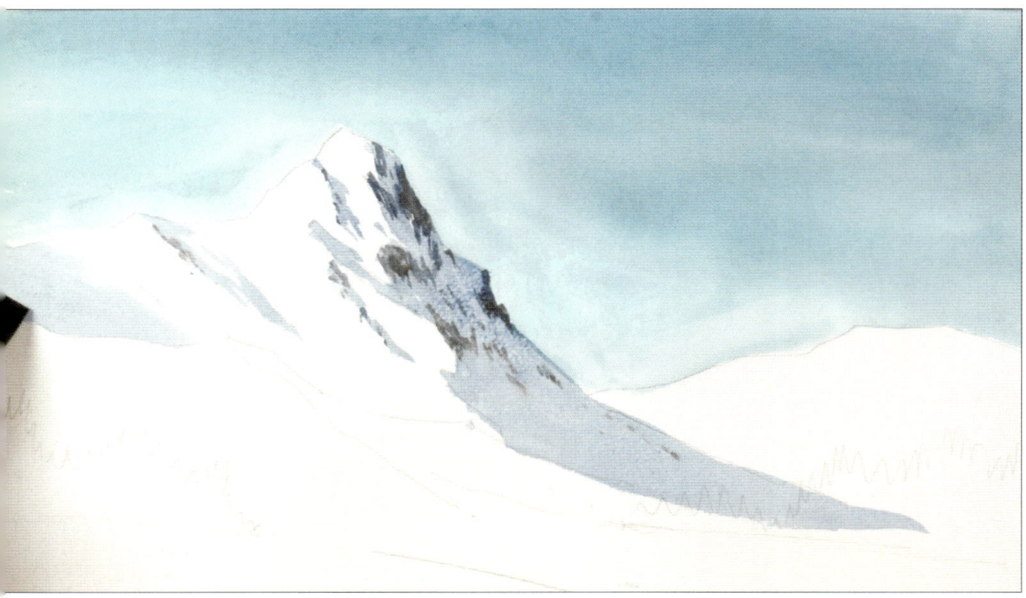

4 When the rocks are dry, make the shadow mix (see right) and use the larger flat brush to put in the shadows on the right-facing slopes of the mountain (the light is coming from the left).

Tip

Shadows in these demonstrations are grey-blue. To produce this colour add to some cobalt blue a tinge of permanent rose (to slightly purple it) and then a tinge of cadmium scarlet (to grey it).

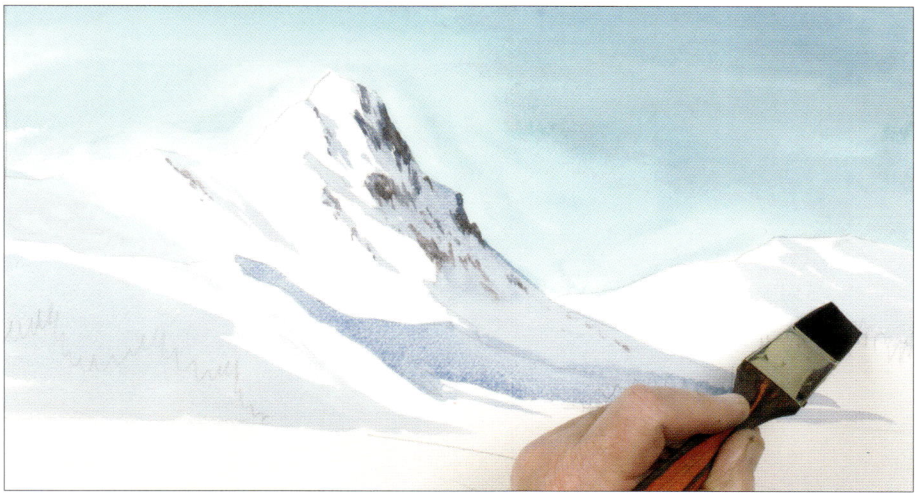

5 Continue laying in the remaining shadows, varying the colour and strength of the mix to create different depths of shadow.

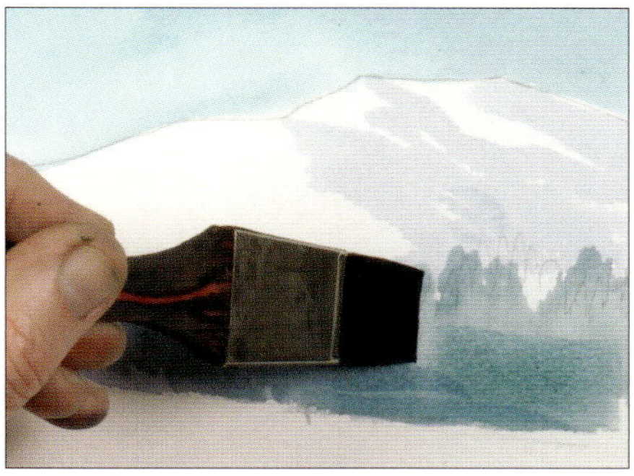

6 Put in the forest at the foot of the mountain on the right-hand side using a blue-green wash of Winsor blue (green shade) mixed with burnt umber. To create the treetops, lay the brush flat against the paper and wiggle it up and down.

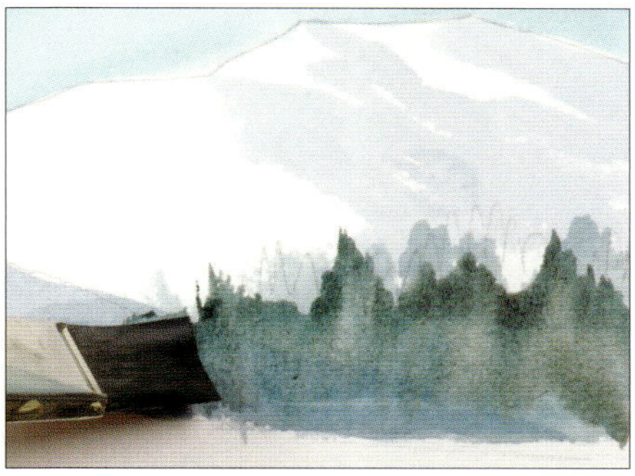

7 Strengthen the mix and place another layer of trees on top of the first. This will push back the first layer and give the forest depth.

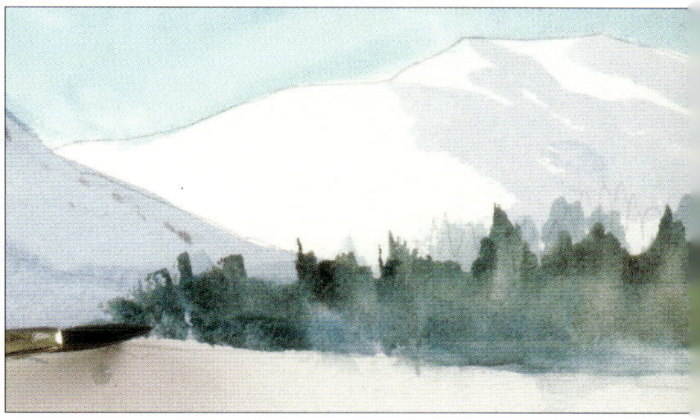

8 Use the edge of the brush to dab in the foliage on the left-hand edge of the forest. Soften the edges with a clean, damp brush.

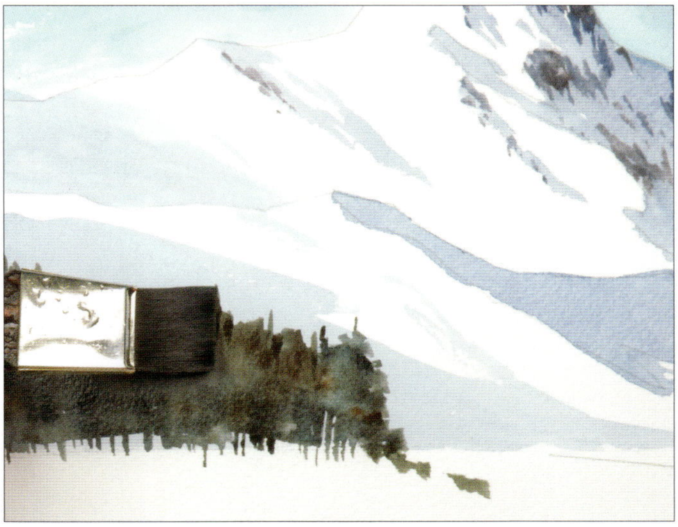

9 Add a little burnt sienna to the mix to warm it up and put in the trees on the left. The warmer colours will bring them forward and push the right-hand trees further back, giving depth to the picture. Use the flat edge of the brush to dab in the tree trunks and to suggest one or two individual trees.

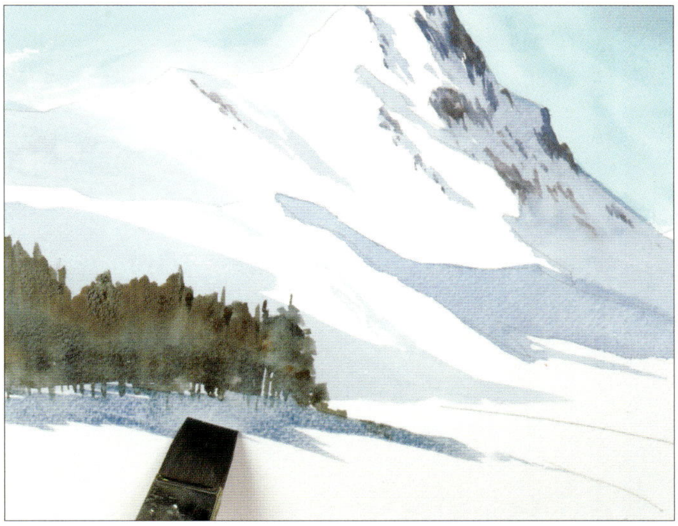

10 Make a little more of the shadow mix (see page 18) and pull down the shadows from the trees.

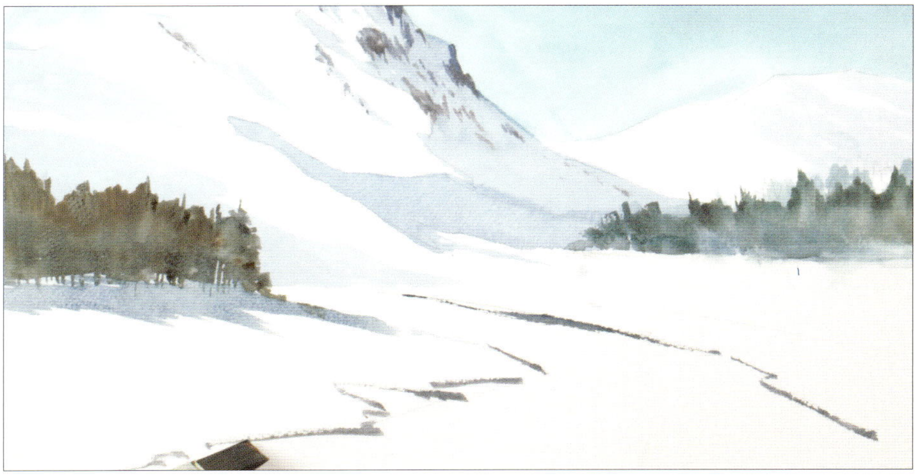

11 Make a dark grey mix of French ultramarine and burnt sienna and drag an uneven line down from the corner of the shadow into the foreground. Drag another line from the foot of the mountain. These lines help break up the foreground and lead the eye into the picture.

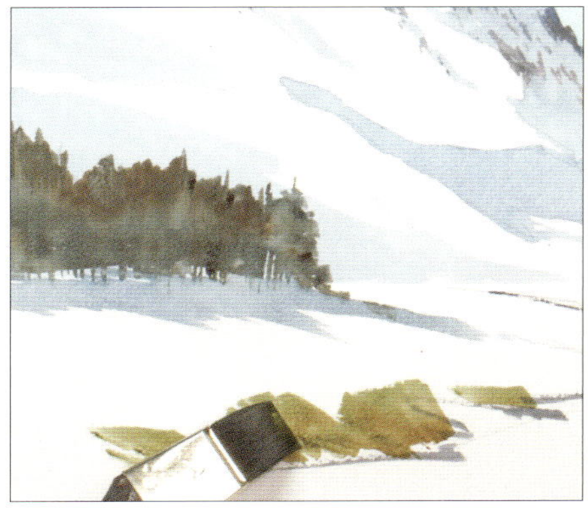

12 Mix some new gamboge and burnt sienna and put in the foreground rocks on the left.

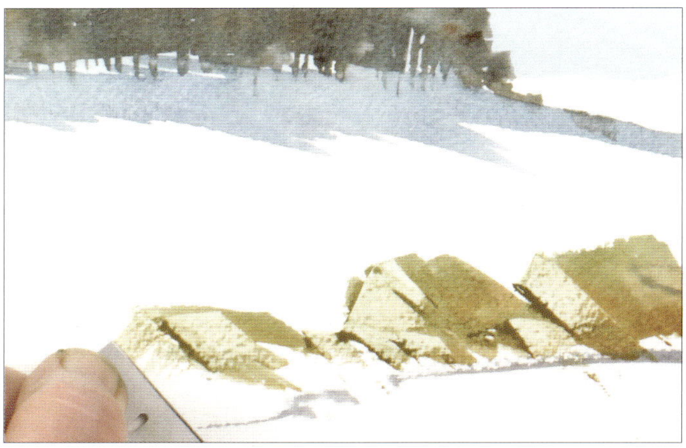

Tip

When using a razor blade to scrape out highlights, make sure the paint is still wet and place the razor blade with the edge flat on the surface. Tilt the blade in the direction you wish to scrape and push the pigment firmly in that direction. Be careful you don't cut yourself – use safety blades, which have a blade on only one side.

13 While the paint is still wet, use a razor blade to scrape away the paint on the left-hand sides of the rocks where the sunlight hits them. The razor blade produces hard edges, mimicking the sharp corners of the rock.

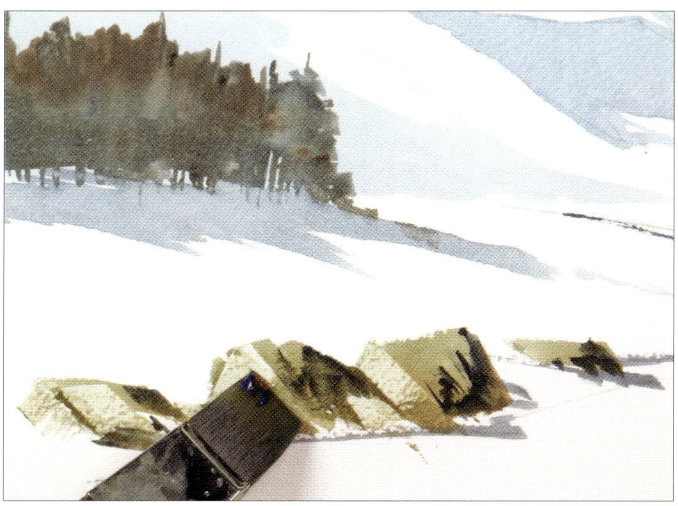

14 Make a mix of burnt sienna and French ultramarine and darken the shadows on the right-hand sides of the rocks.

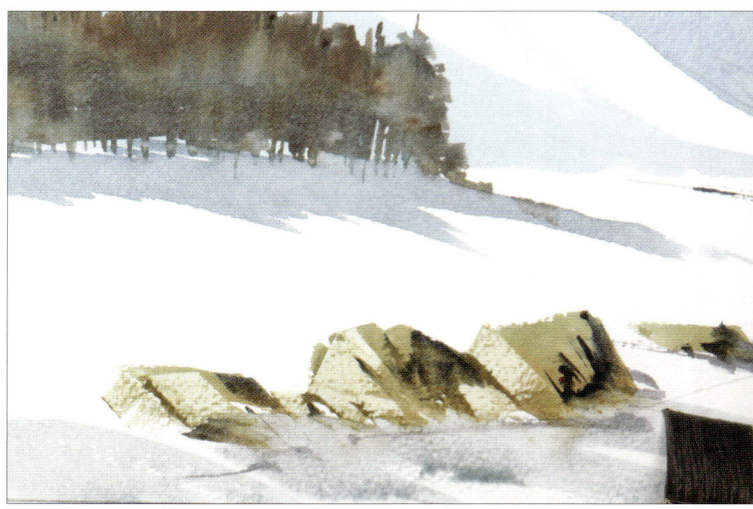

15 Using the shadow mix (see steps 4 and 10), put in the shadows around the rocks on the snow.

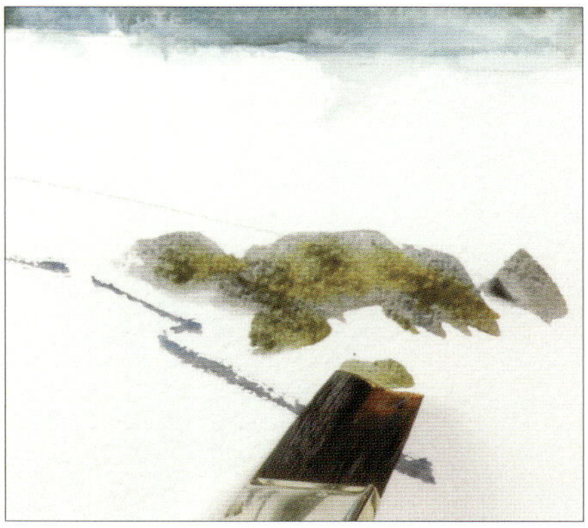

16 Use the same mix as before to put in the rocks on the right.

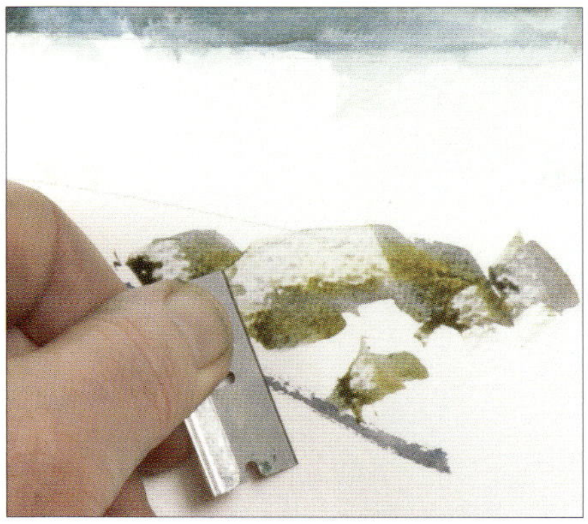

17 Scrape away the paint to create highlights using the razor blade.

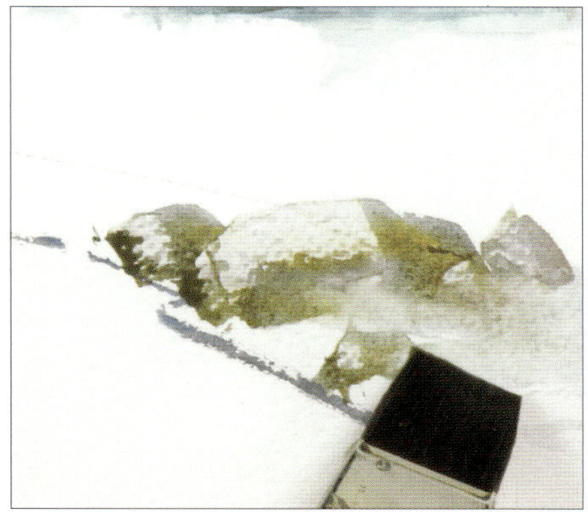

18 Put in the shadows below the rocks.

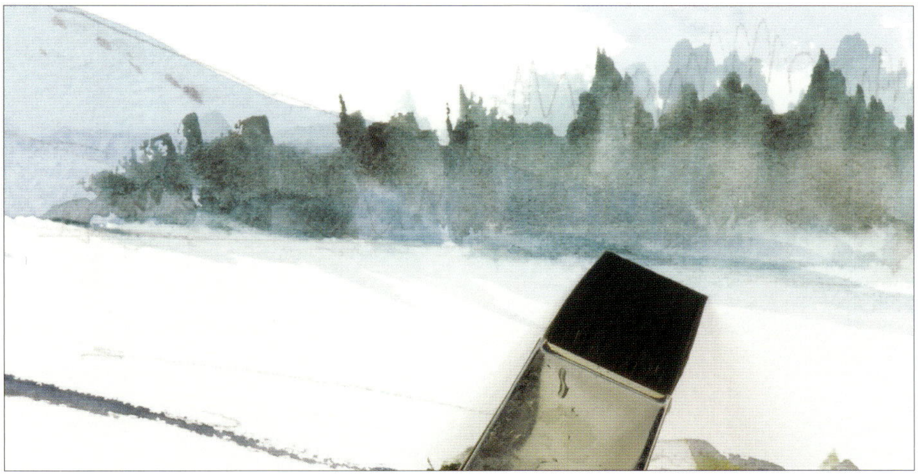

19 Also place the shadows beneath the trees on the right.

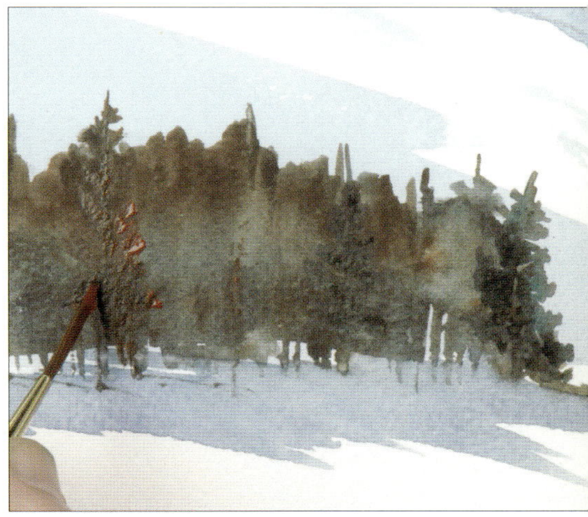

20 Using the no. 3 rigger, add some details to one or two of the foreground trees on the left of the picture. This adds texture and brings the trees further forward. Use a strong mix of burnt sienna and Winsor blue (green shade).

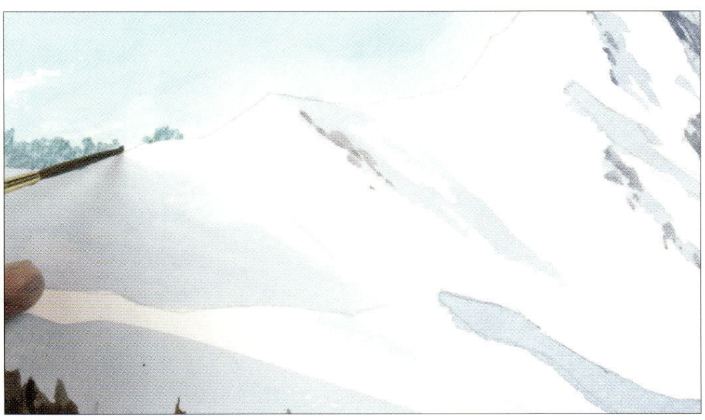

21 Make a small quantity of Winsor blue (green shade) mixed with burnt umber and dot in some distant trees at the top of the slope on the left.

22 When the painting is completely dry, remove any visible lines using a putty eraser.

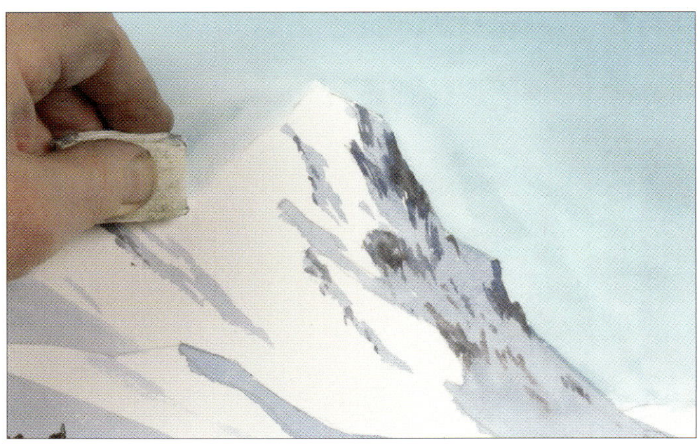

Overleaf

The finished painting.

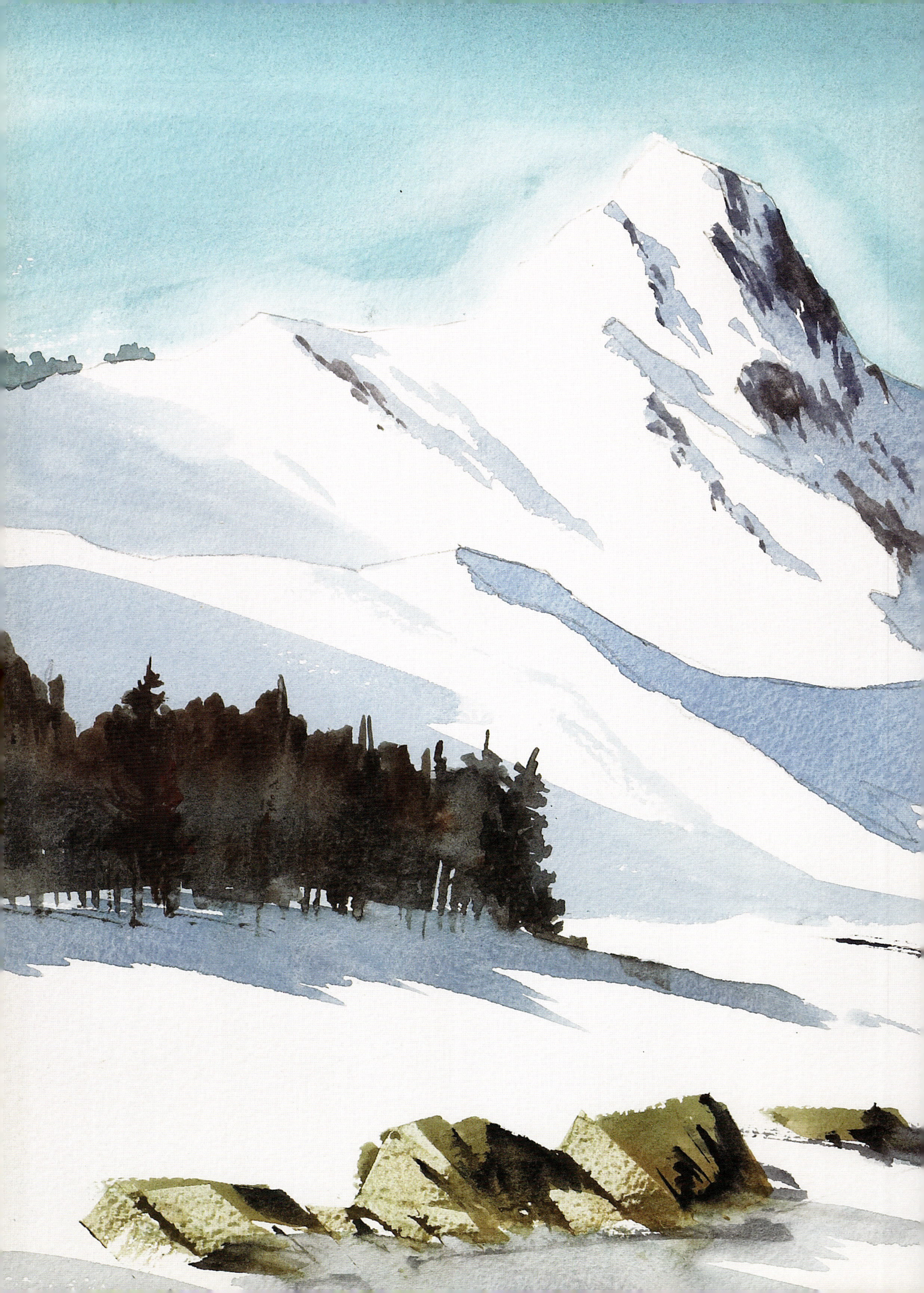

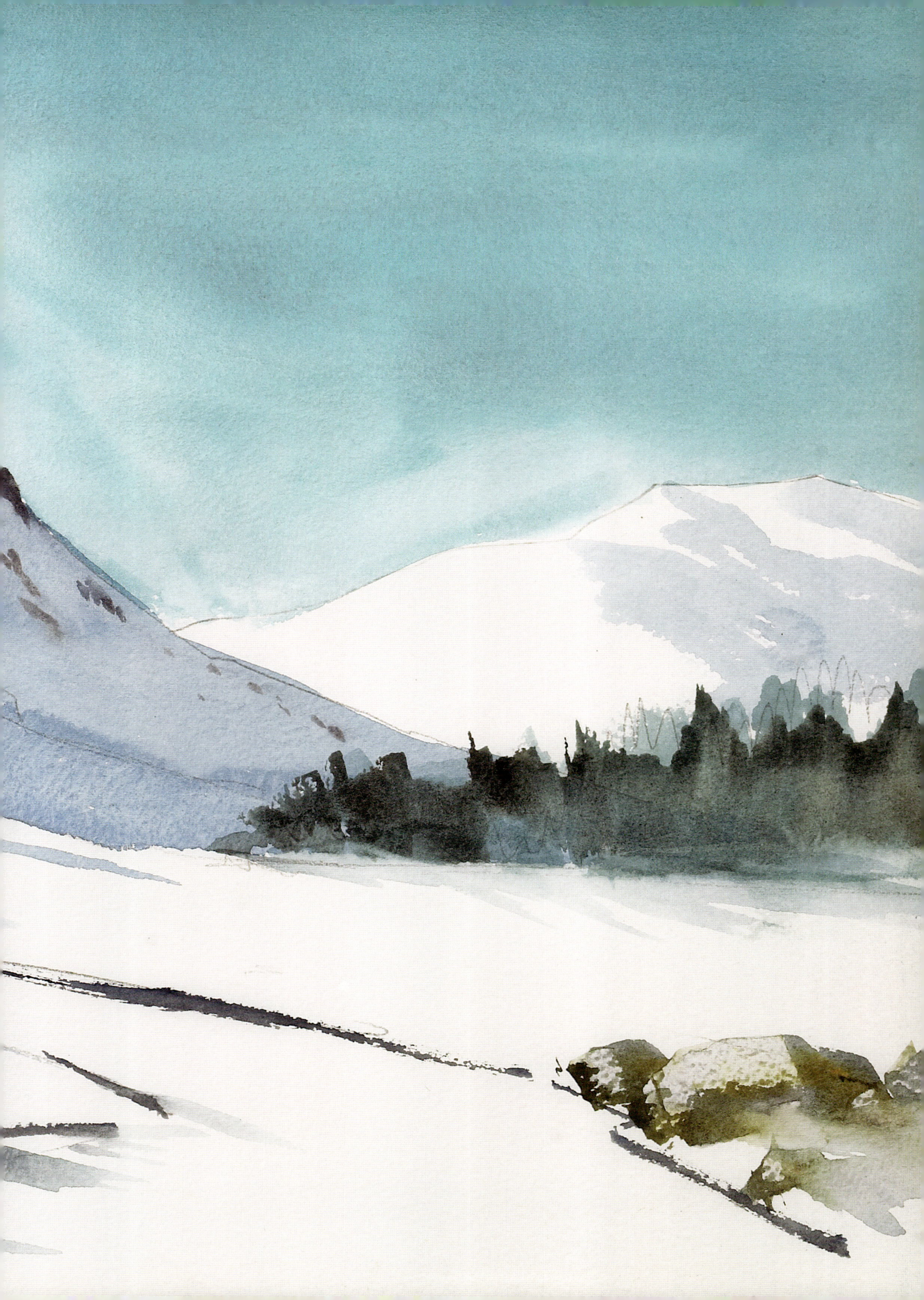

Water's Edge

TRACING
4

The light is coming from the left in this painting, so I have scraped out some strata on the cliff face to indicate this. I have painted the cliff face using a number of different colours to enliven the painting and add interest. The lake was added so that I could include some reflections of the landscape, and to create a gentle area as a foil to the hard, textured cliff face.

You will need

180gsm (90lb) NOT watercolour paper
Kneadable (putty) eraser
Safety razor blade
Kitchen paper
Small piece of sponge
Brushes: 25mm (1in) flat brush; 13mm (½in) flat brush with a scraper end; no. 3 rigger
Paints: manganese blue hue, cadmium scarlet, cobalt blue, French ultramarine, cadmium lemon, new gamboge, cadmium orange, burnt sienna and permanent rose

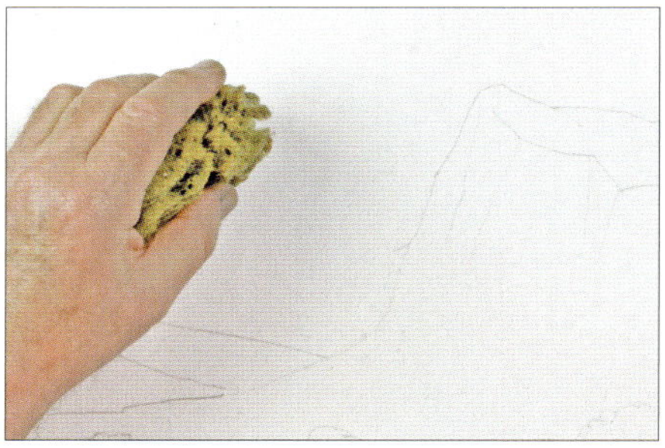

1 Begin in the usual way by dampening the sky area using a damp sponge. Take the water right down to the horizon. Avoid over-wetting the paper.

2 Mix up some manganese blue hue and lay on the lower part of the sky using the 25mm (1in) flat brush. Blend out the paint to a paler shade as you move from the top of the sky to the bottom. Move the brush in all directions to avoid streaking.

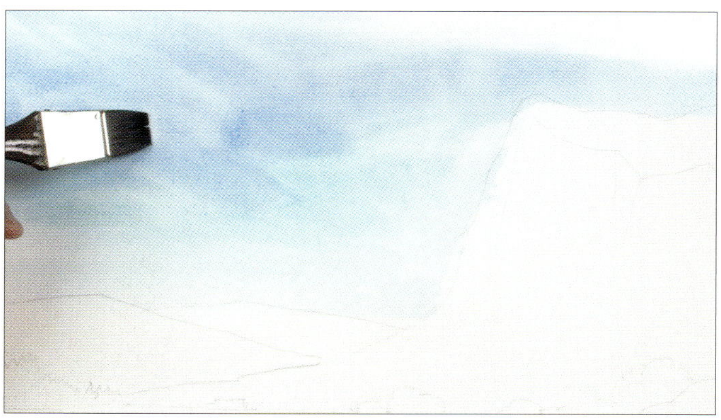

3 For the upper part of the sky use cobalt blue, which is a warmer blue. Blend the two colours together where they meet.

4 At the top of the sky, use French ultramarine mixed with a tiny amount of cadmium scarlet. Blend all the colours together seamlessly to create a gradation from warm to cool blue as you move down the picture.

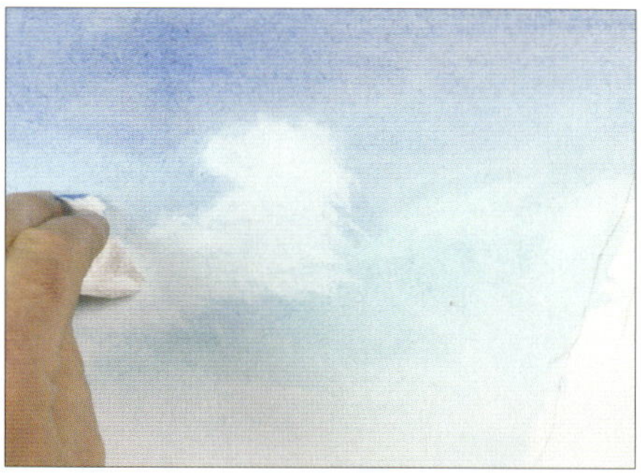

5 Lift out some wispy clouds by dabbing the wet paint with a screwed-up piece of kitchen paper. Turn the piece of paper continuously to avoid putting back in the paint you have picked up.

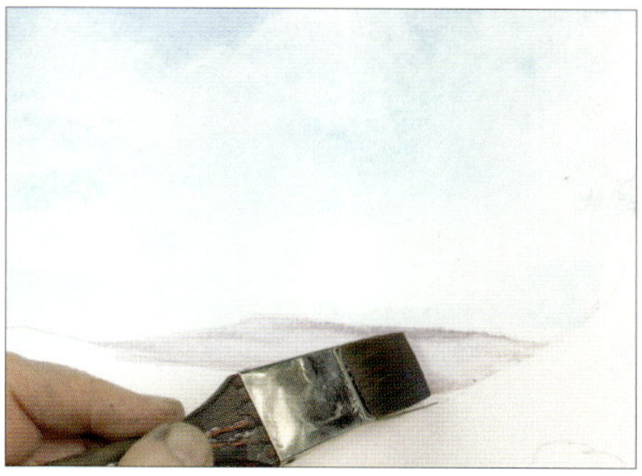

6 Make a dry mix of cobalt blue and cadmium scarlet. Re-wet the distant hills, wring out the brush and pick up some colour using a single brushstroke. Place the colour on the top of the furthest hills.

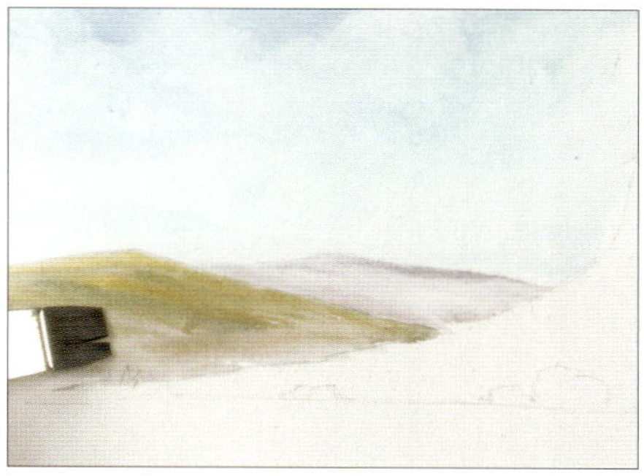

7 Add some new gamboge to the mix and paint the hills in front. Thin the mix down towards the base of the hills. Using a warmer colour as you move towards the foreground will help advance the painting and give it depth.

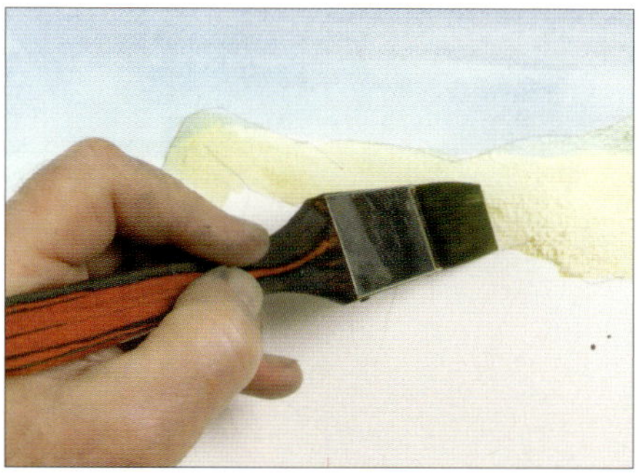

8 Turning to the land at the top of the main mountain on the right, apply a wash of cadmium lemon mixed with a touch of French ultramarine.

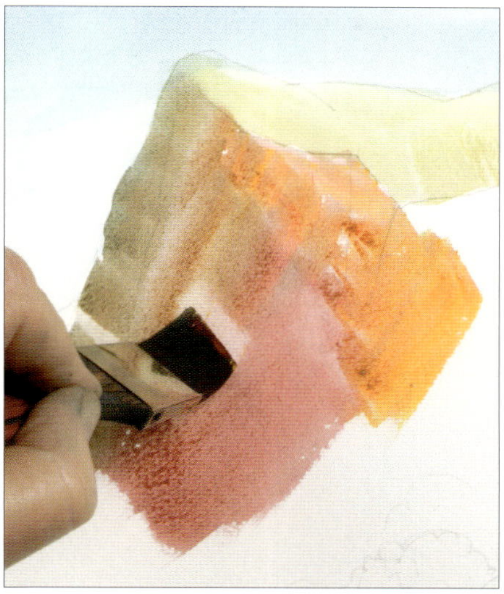

9 Continue painting the cliff face down towards the base of the mountain using a variety of colours. Work quickly, so that the colours blend freely on the paper. Begin with a mix of burnt sienna and cobalt blue, then bring in some permanent rose and some new gamboge.

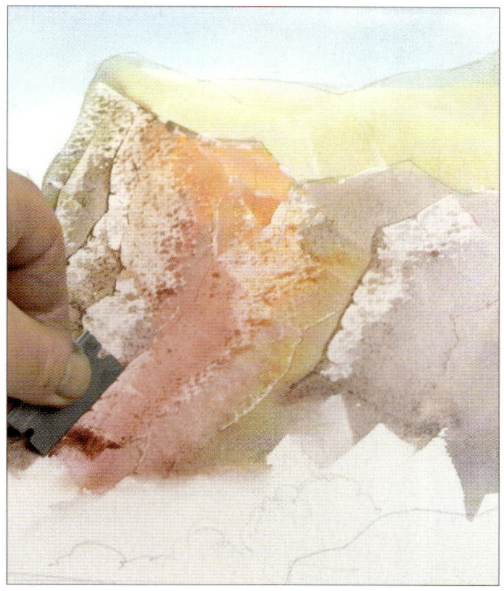

10 Paint the right-hand side of the mountain using the burnt sienna and cobalt blue mix. While the paint is still wet, scrape out the colour using a razor blade to create areas of light (see page 20). These will help define the cliff and give it texture.

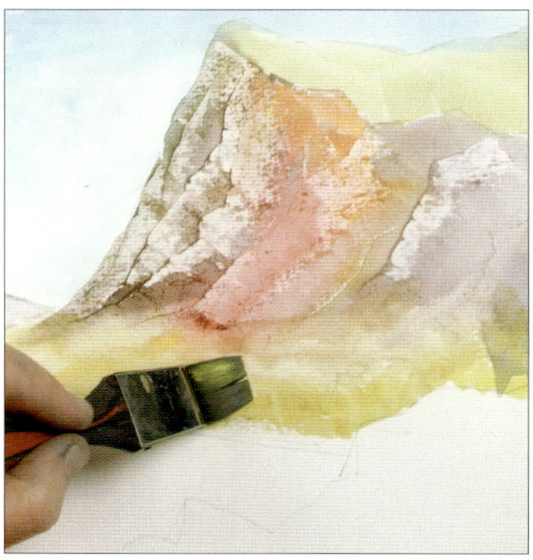

11 Lay a wash of cadmium lemon at the foot of the mountain and blend it into the colours above it.

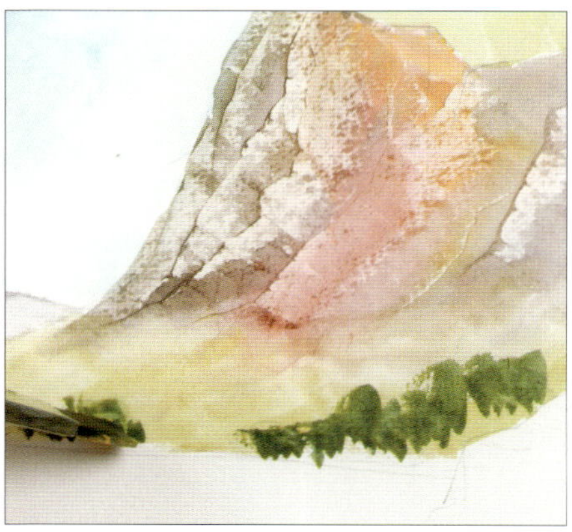

12 Make a strong mix of new gamboge and French ultramarine and put in the trees at the foot of the mountain. Use the corner of the brush and wiggle it up and down to form the shape of the trees.

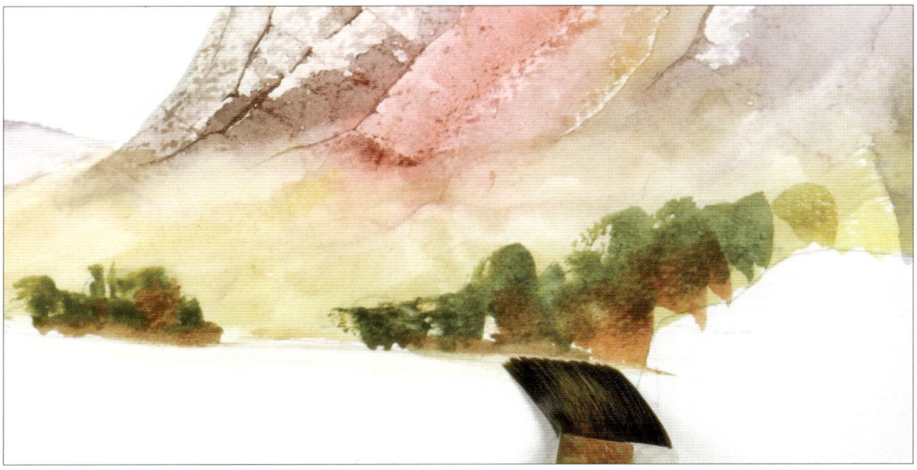

Tip

Place complementary colours, such as red and green, next to each other to enliven and add richness to a painting.

13 While the paint is still wet, put a suggestion of burnt sienna into the green. Straighten the line at the base of the trees with a clean, damp brush.

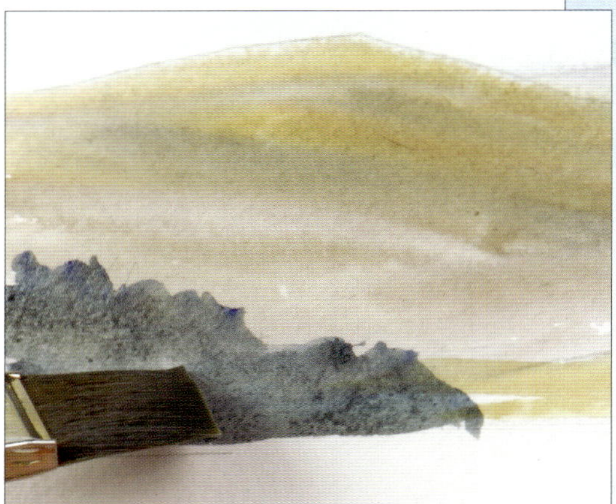

14 Mix some French ultramarine into the green to cool it down and put in the distant trees on the left. Soften the lower edge of the paint if necessary.

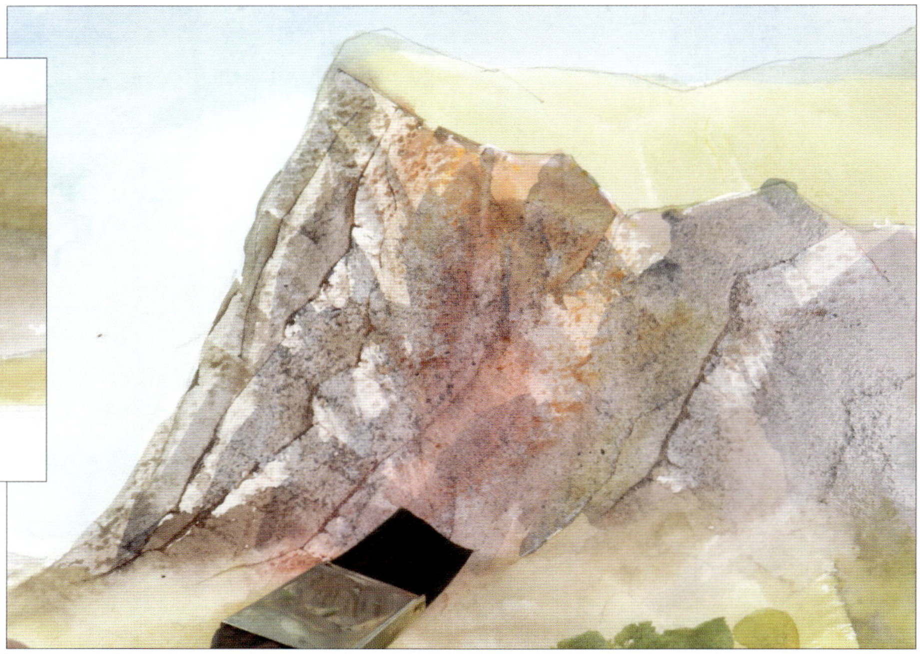

15 Make the purple-grey shadow mix (see page 18) and lay strong shadows diagonally across the cliff face. This will break up the hard edges and put more light into the rocks (the sun is coming from the left).

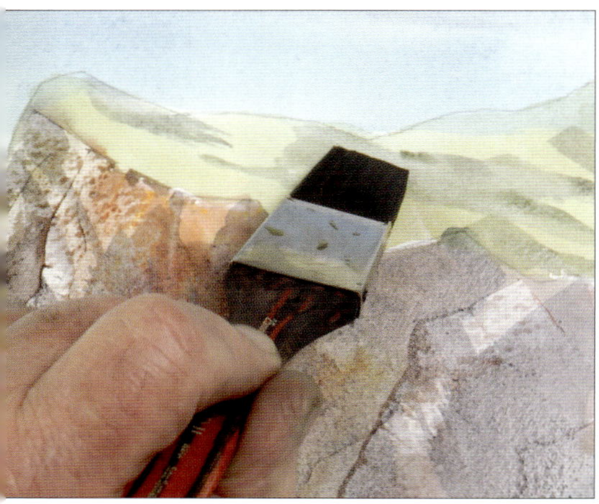

16 Lay some shadows across the land at the top of the mountain too. Soften them with a clean, damp brush.

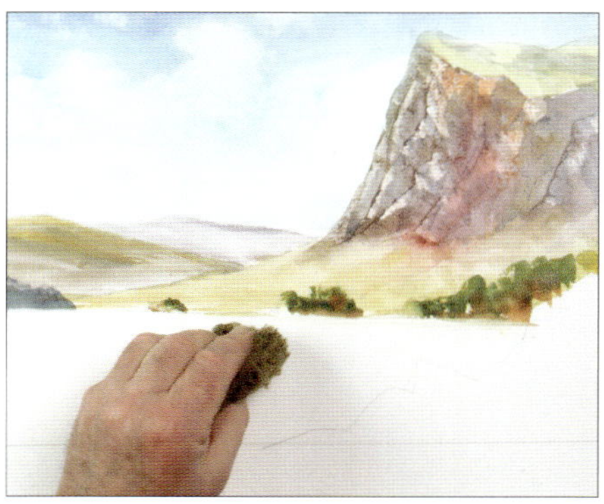

17 Re-wet the lake area with a damp sponge.

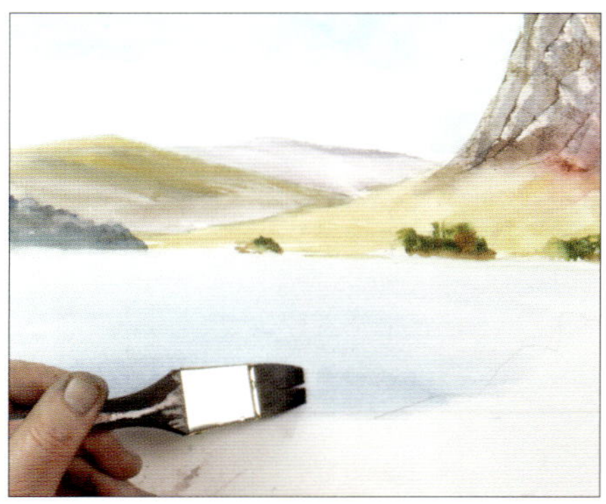

18 Brush in some cobalt blue at the top of the lake, where it reflects the sky.

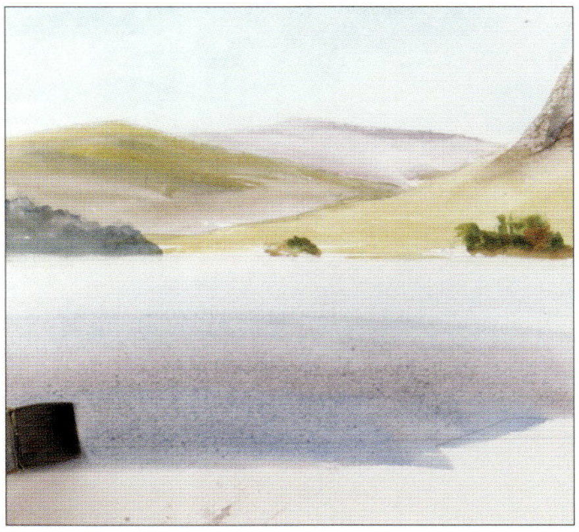

19 Blend in a mix of French ultramarine and cadmium scarlet at the bottom.

Tip

Water reflects the colour of the sky, so use the same colours in each to link them together and create a more realistic picture. In general, always paint reflections using the same colours as the object being reflected.

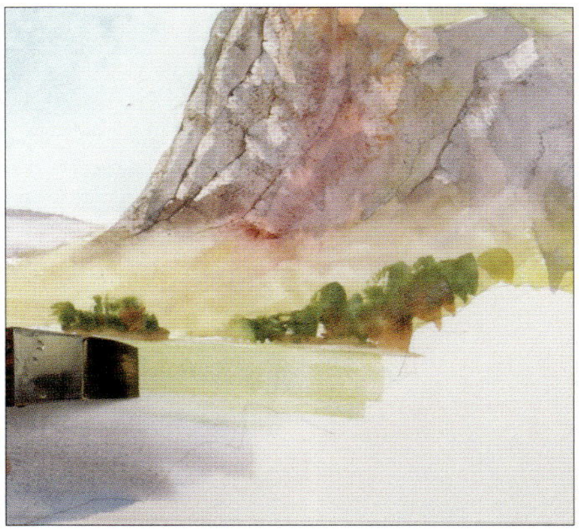

20 While the paint is still wet, put in some new gamboge on the left, below the mountain.

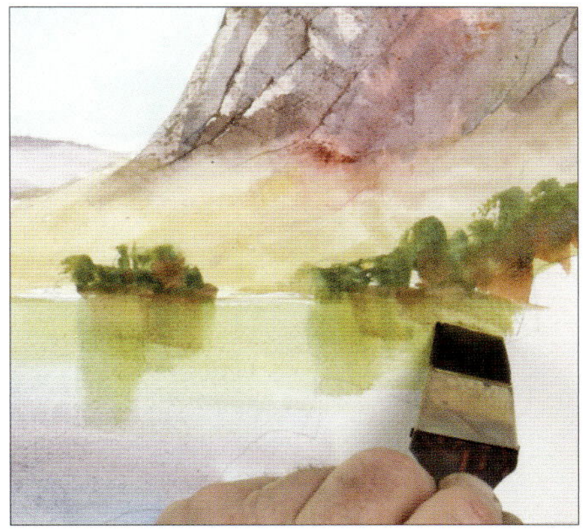

21 Using undiluted French ultramarine mixed with new gamboge, pull down the reflections from the trees. Add a little burnt sienna into the reflections too.

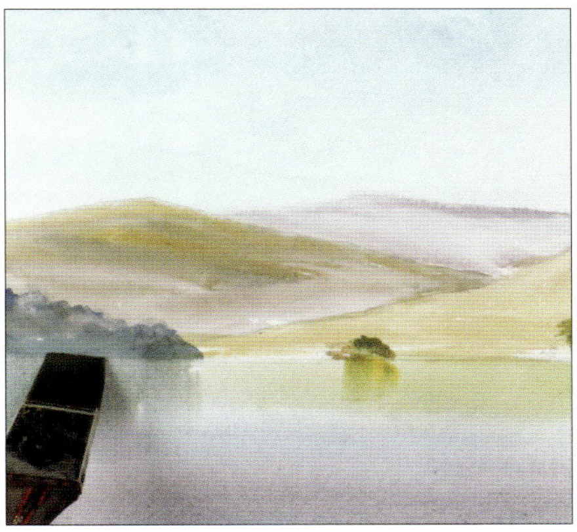

22 Pull some green down from the trees on the left. Use the same mix for the reflections as you used for the trees.

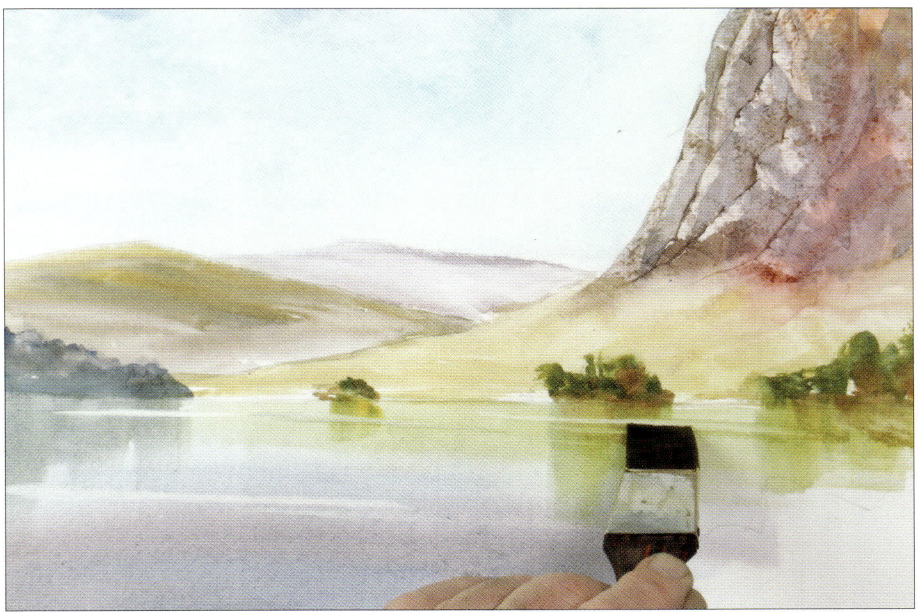

23 Using a clean, damp brush, put in some ripples on the water surface by dragging the flat edge of the brush horizontally through the wet paint.

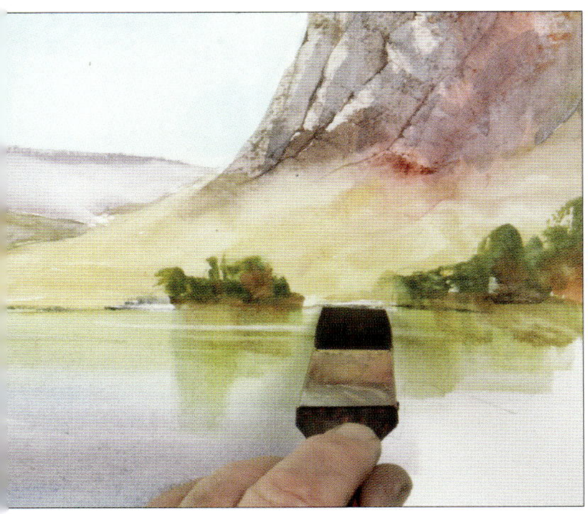

24 Dab some French ultramarine and burnt sienna along the edge of the lake to define it.

Tip

When creating ripples, ensure there is less water in the brush than on the paper. The water will then be drawn from the paper to the brush. Move the edge of the brush horizontally across the wet paint to create ripples.

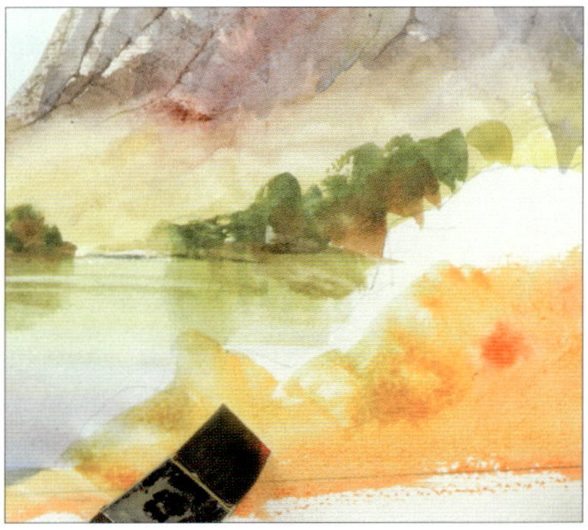

25 Place the rocks on the right-hand side in the foreground by dabbing in first some cadmium orange and then cadmium scarlet.

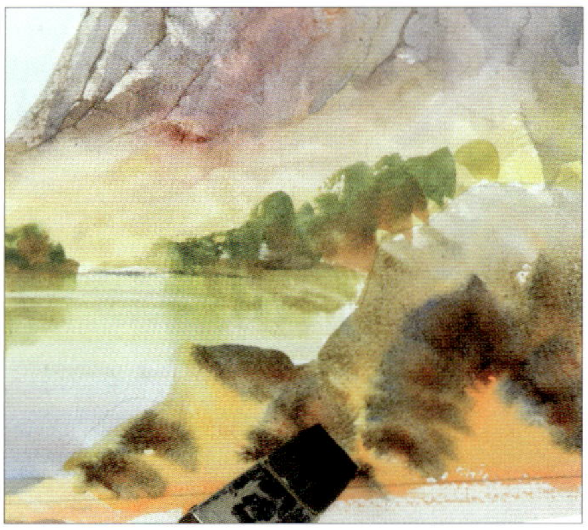

26 While the paint is still wet, drop in some French ultramarine and some burnt sienna. Allow the colours to mix together on the paper.

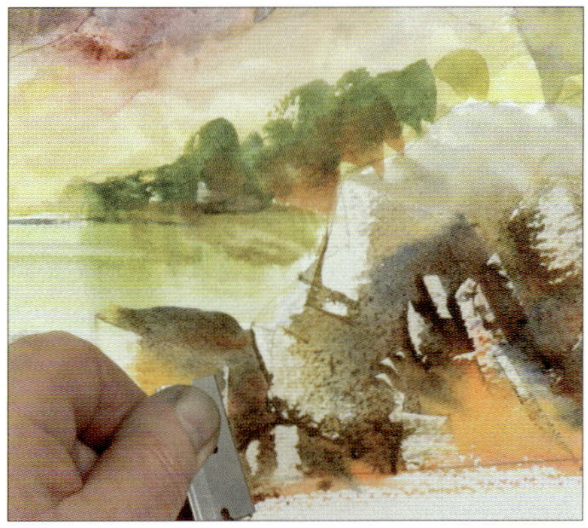

27 Scrape out the paint with the razor blade to create light areas and define the shapes of the rocks.

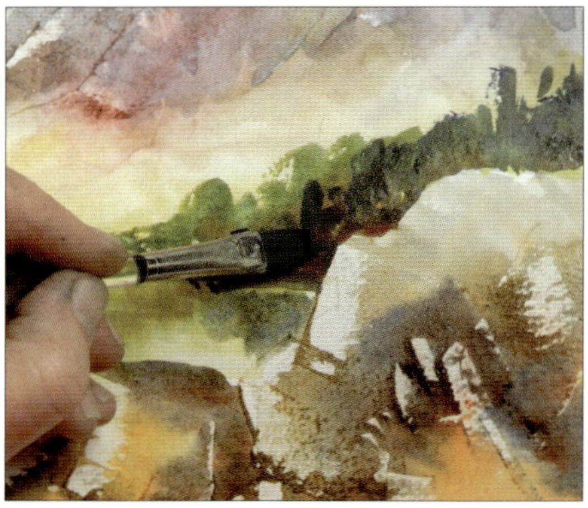

28 Change to the smaller flat brush and darken the area behind the rocks. Use a mix of cadmium scarlet and French ultramarine. Use the same colour to strengthen the reflections in the water.

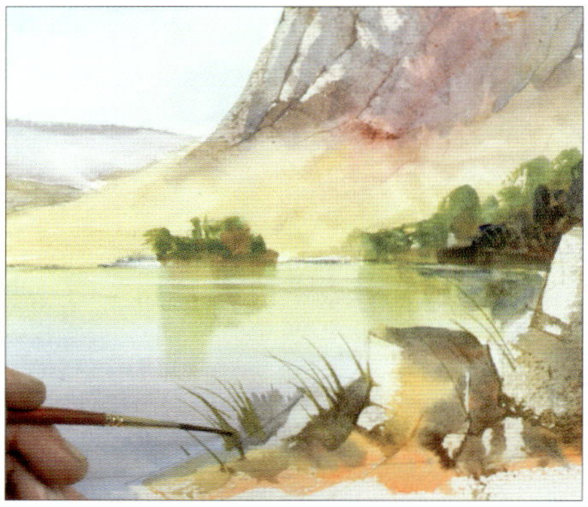

29 Using the same mix, paint in some grasses around the rocks at the water's edge. Drop in the paint, then use the no. 3 rigger to pull out the grass stems.

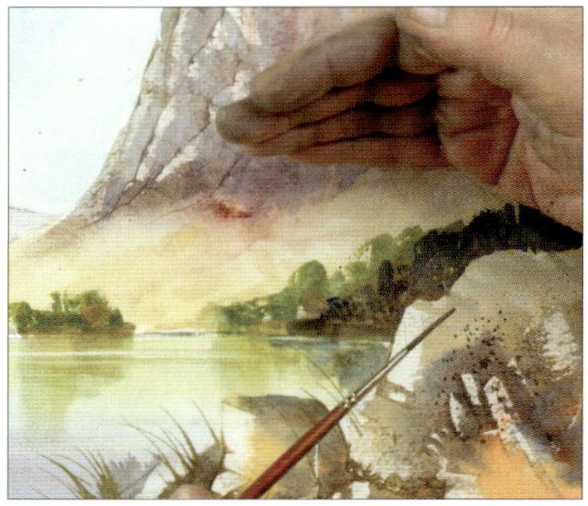

30 Shielding the rest of the picture with your hand, splatter in some paint by flicking it off the brush with your finger. This is a good way of adding texture to the rocks.

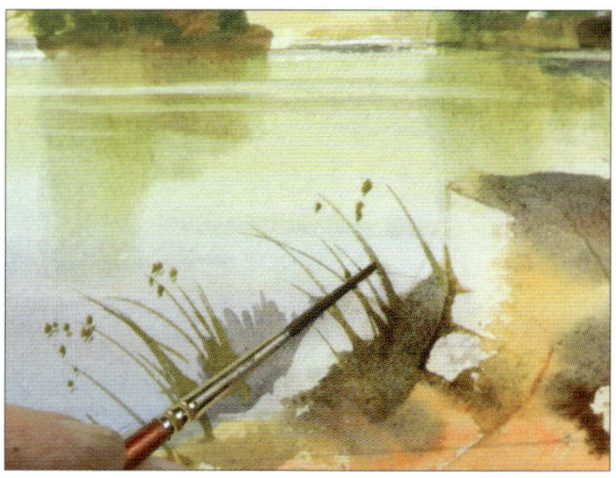

31 Dab in some flowerheads around the ends of the grasses. Any colour will do for this, though I have used the same mix as I used for the grasses.

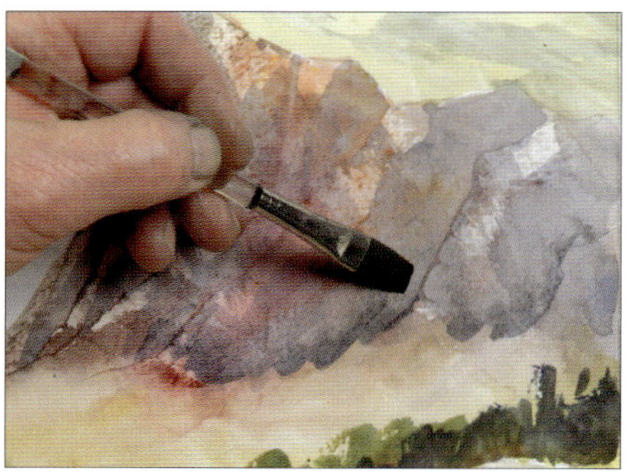

32 Mix French ultramarine and burnt sienna, and use the smaller flat brush to strengthen the shadows at the base of the cliff. Soften with a clean, damp brush.

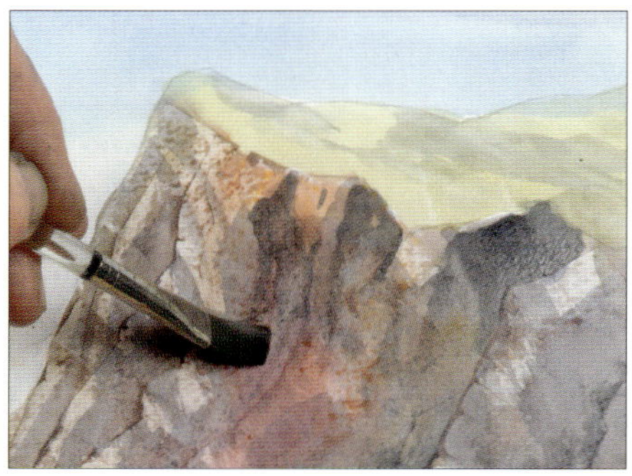

33 Strengthen the shadows at the top of the cliff in the same way.

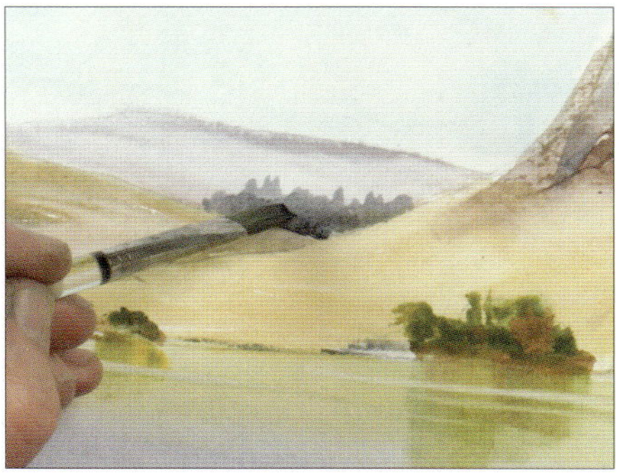

34 Make a mix of French ultramarine and a little new gamboge and put in the suggestion of a forest at the base of the distant hill. This will strengthen the background and lighten the hilltop, pushing it further into the distance.

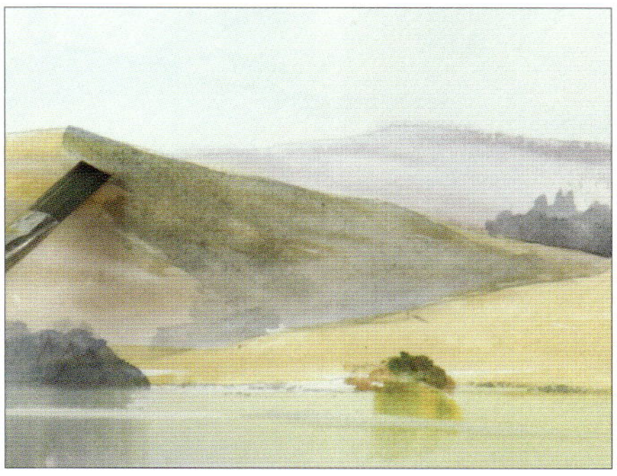

35 Strengthen the shadow on the right-facing side of the mid-ground hill using the shadow mix (see step 15).

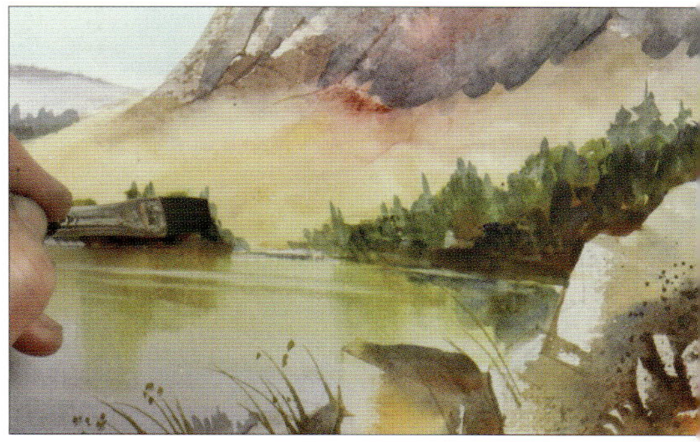

36 Add definition to the forest on the right by painting in a few individual trees using the edge of the brush and a mix of French ultramarine and new gamboge. Space out the trees unevenly so that they do not appear too regimented.

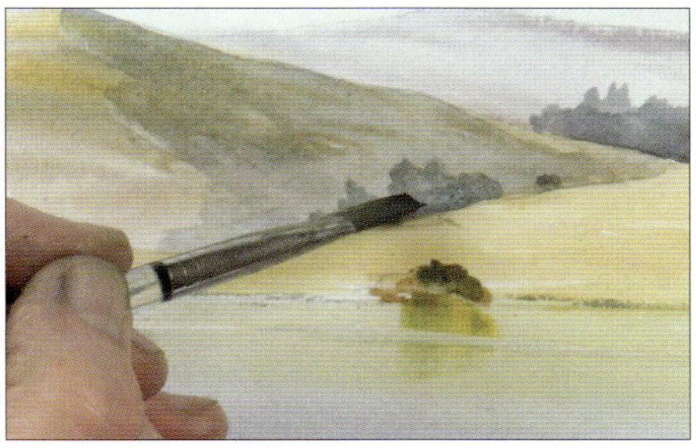

37 Using the same mix as in step 34, put in a few more trees to better define the mid-ground.

38 Knock back the red on the cliff face by laying a grey-blue wash of cobalt blue and some burnt sienna over the top. Use the same mix to add more shadows to the ground at the foot of the mountain and soften them in.

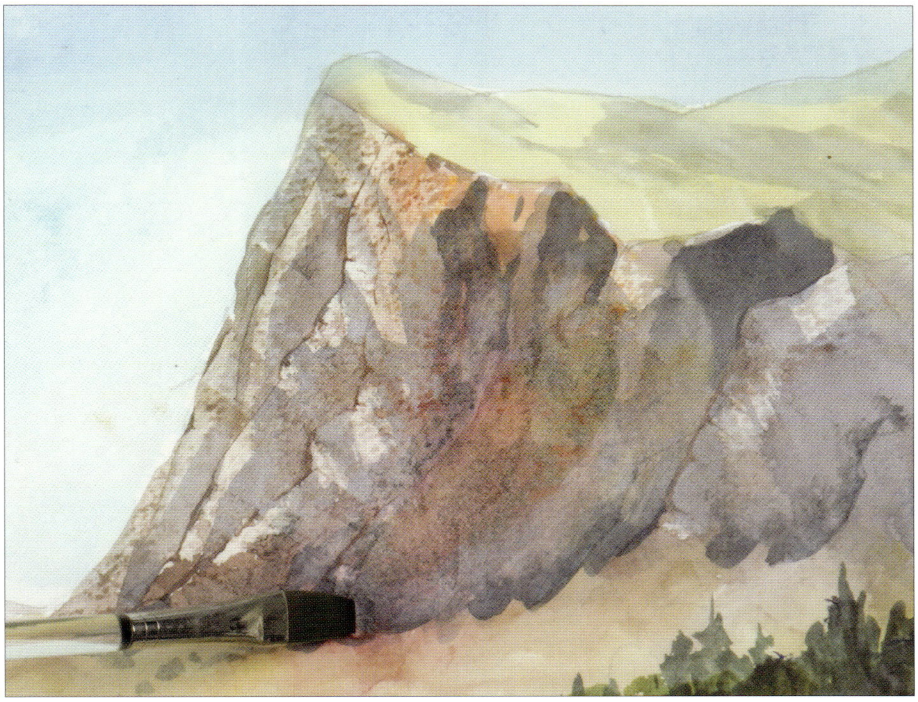

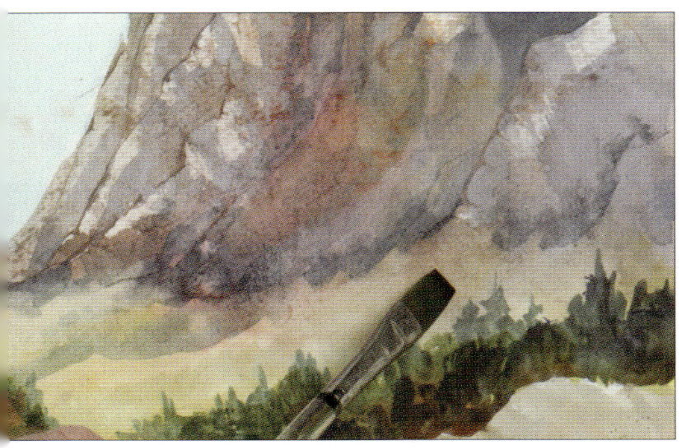

39 Lay the blue-grey wash over the area at the bottom of the cliff to subdue it.

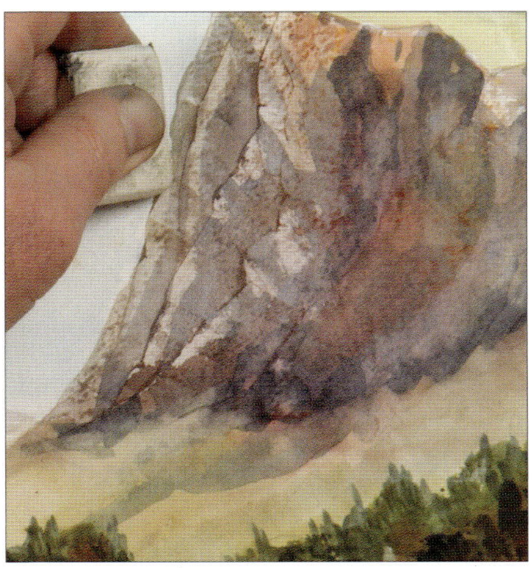

40 When the painting is completely dry, remove any visible lines using a putty eraser.

Overleaf

The finished painting.

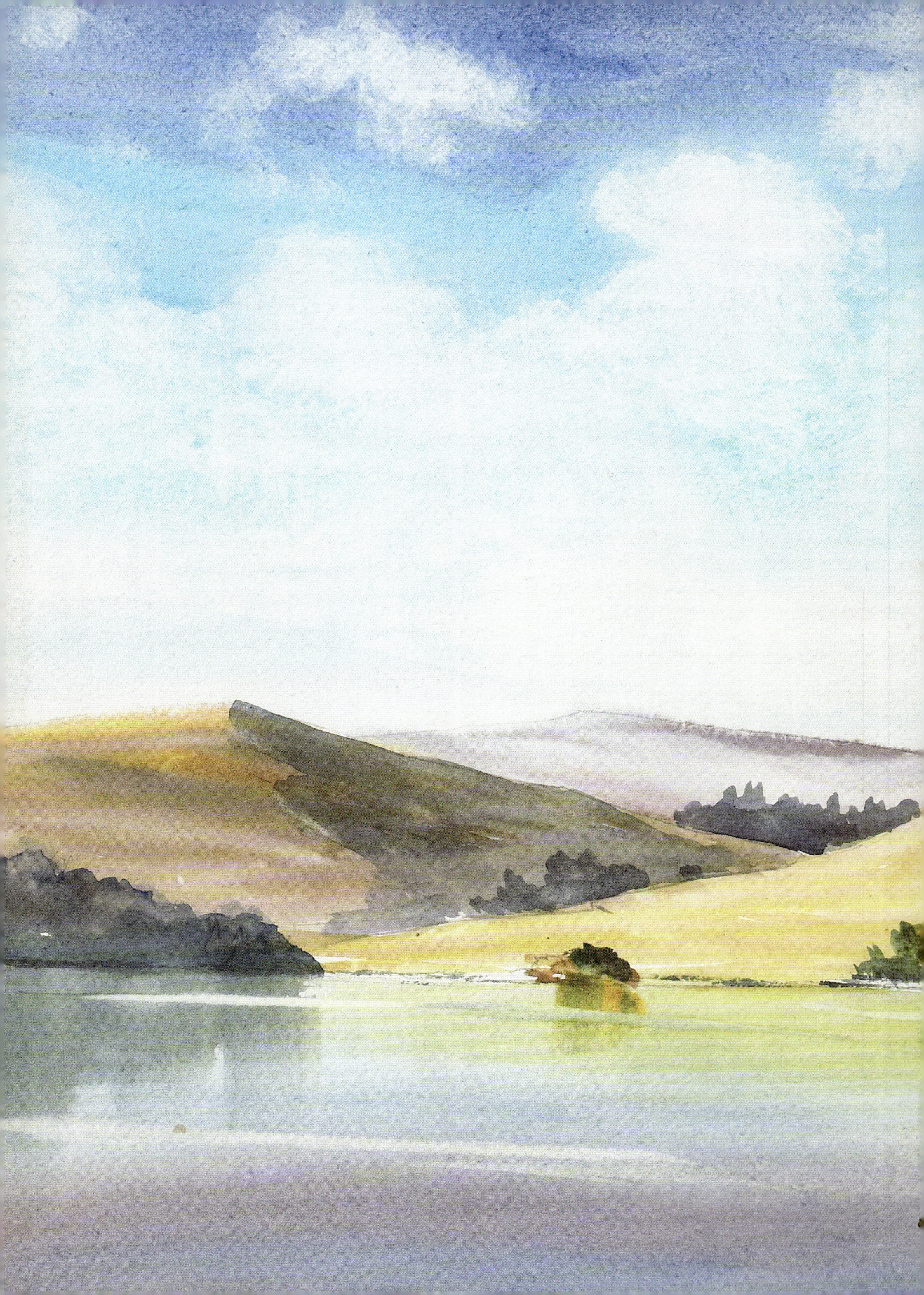

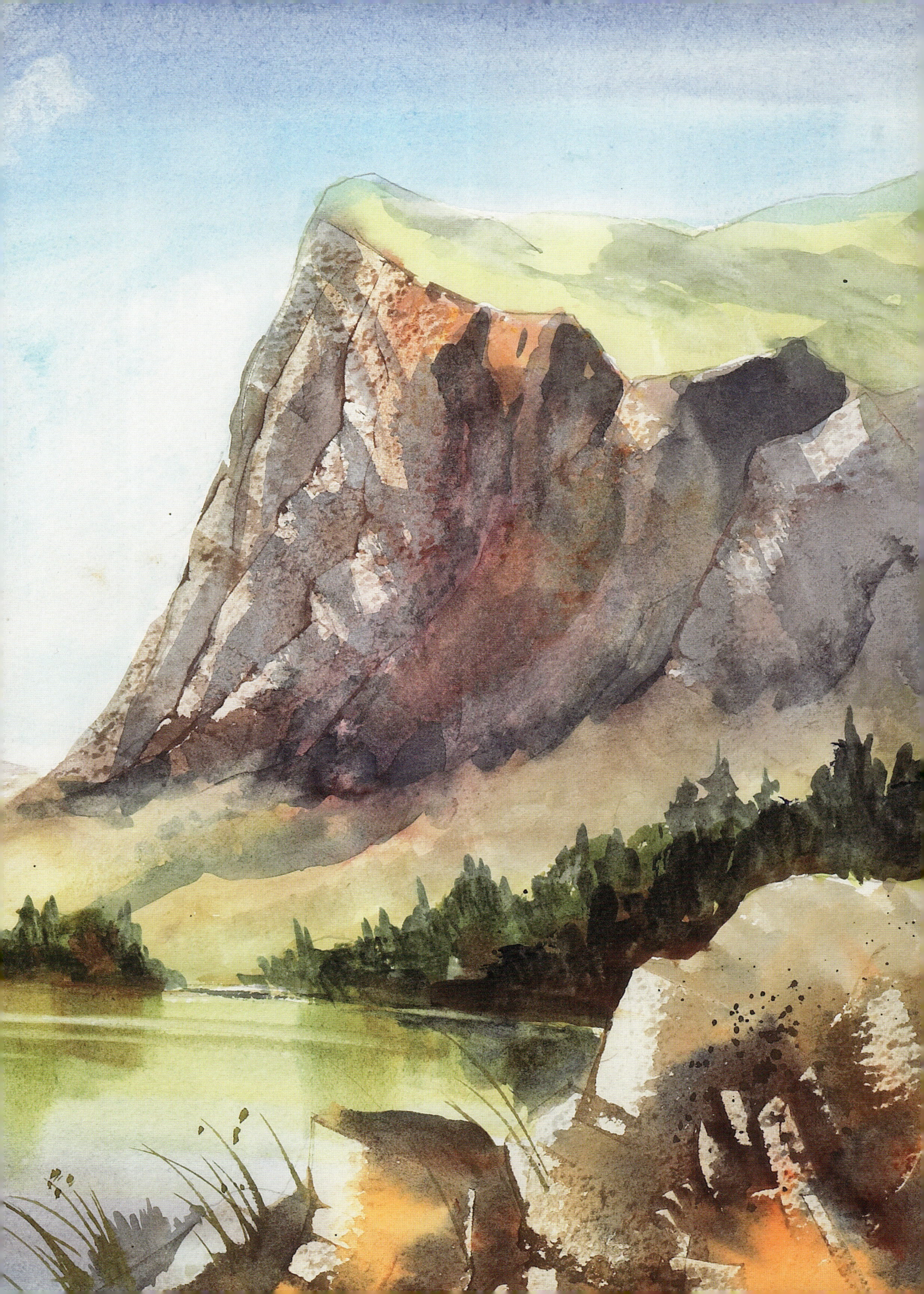

Castle on the Cliffs

TRACING 5

The castle dominates this painting, so I have given it a distinctive shape. I have used perspective to emphasise its height above the cliffs, and this effect is further enhanced by the low horizon. Cooler colours in the distant hills and warmer colours in the cliff face and foreground are used to create depth.

You will need

- 180gsm (90lb) NOT watercolour paper
- Kneadable (putty) eraser
- Safety razor blade
- Kitchen paper
- Brushes: 25mm (1in) flat brush; 13mm (½in) flat brush with a scraper end; no. 3 rigger
- Paints: cobalt blue, French ultramarine, cadmium scarlet, new gamboge, cadmium lemon, permanent rose, burnt sienna, burnt umber and cadmium orange

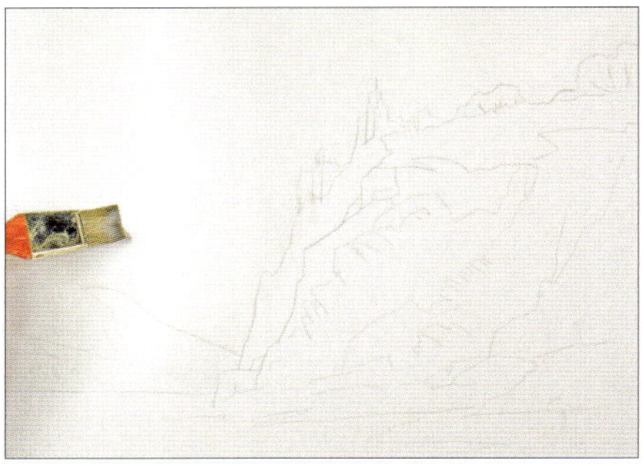

1 Begin by dampening the paper all over using the 25mm (1in) flat brush.

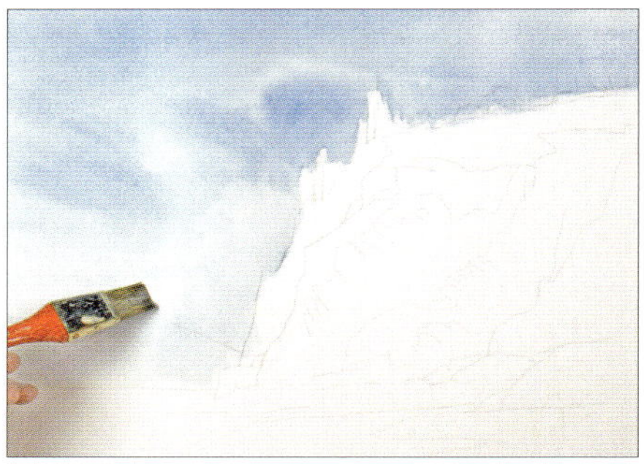

2 While the paper is still wet, use the same brush to lay a wash of cobalt blue over the sky. Blend it out so that it is darker at the top than at the bottom.

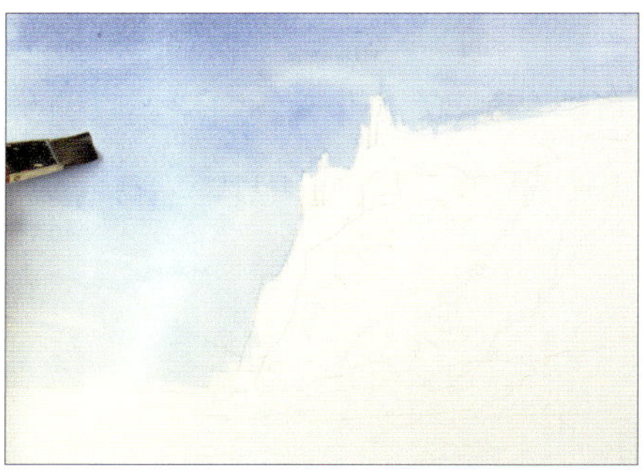

3 Make a mix of French ultramarine and cadmium scarlet and lay this over the top part of the sky to darken it further.

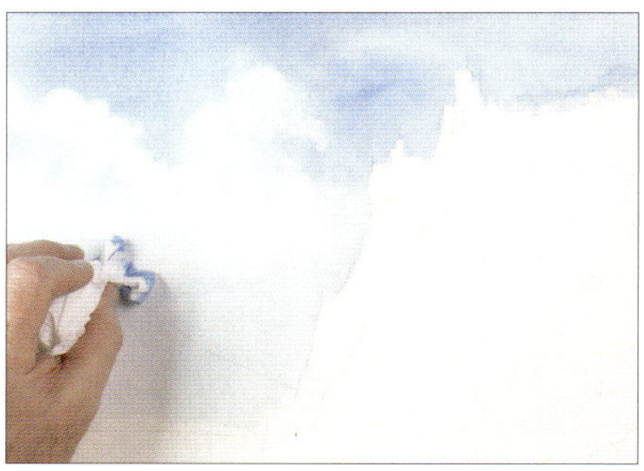

4 Dab out a suggestion of clouds using a crumpled piece of dry kitchen paper. Turn the piece of paper continuously to avoid putting back in the paint you have picked up.

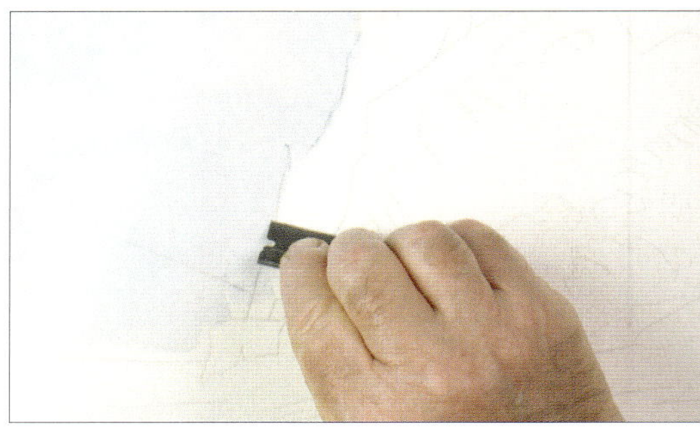

5 Sharpen the edge of the cliff face by scraping away the paint using a razor blade.

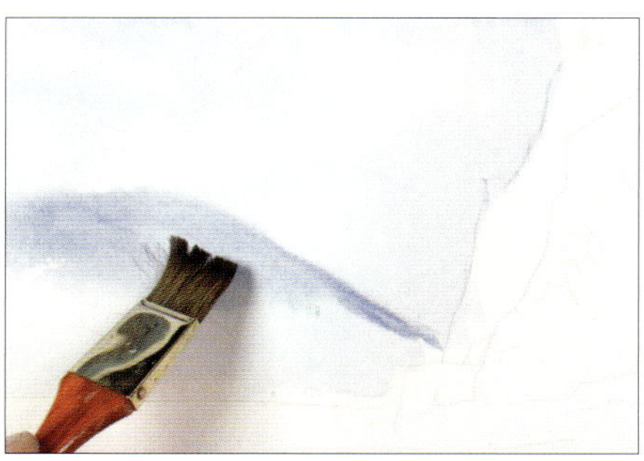

6 While the paint is still wet, make a mix of French ultramarine and cadmium scarlet. Wring out the brush and pick up the paint with a single stroke (this ensures there is just the right amount of water on the brush). Put in the distant mountain on the left.

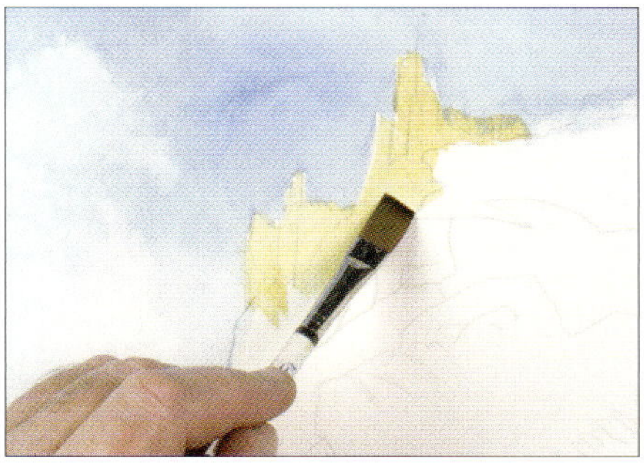

7 When the sky is dry, make a very pale mix of new gamboge and a touch of cadmium scarlet and paint in the castle using the smaller flat brush. Go around the outline carefully.

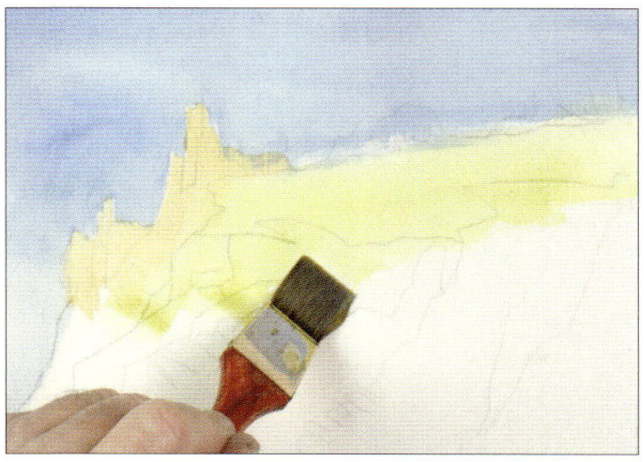

8 Change back to the 25mm (1in) flat brush, add some cadmium lemon to the mix and paint in the top of the cliffs.

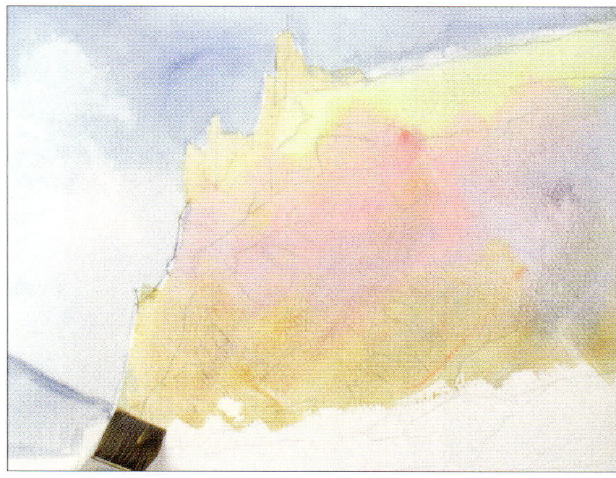

9 Continue painting the cliffs, using first permanent rose, followed by cobalt blue and then new gamboge. Work quickly, blending the colours on the paper while the paint is still wet.

Tip

Always clean your palette with a damp kitchen sponge and wash out your brush between colours.

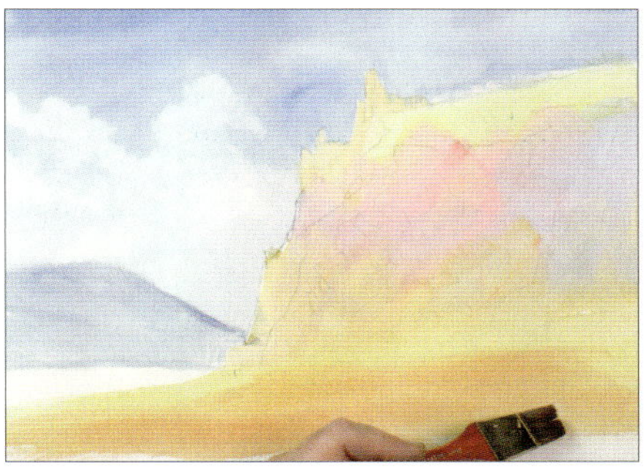

10 Paint in the ground at the bottom of the cliff using first cadmium lemon, followed by a layer of new gamboge, then finish with burnt sienna along the base of the picture. As before, work quickly and blend the colours on the paper. Use long, sweeping brushstrokes.

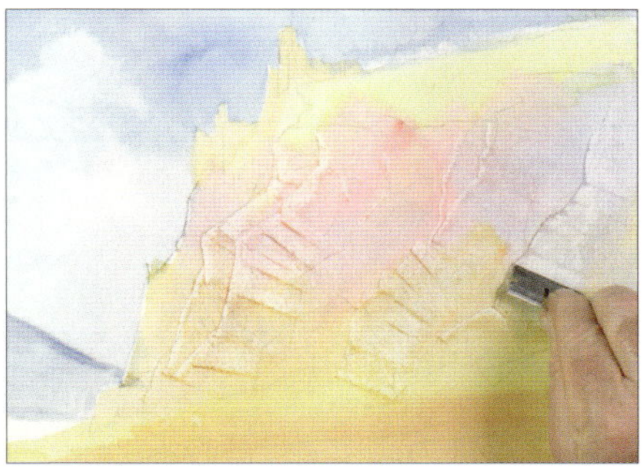

11 Working your way from left to right across the painting, and while the paint is still wet, scrape out the shapes of the rocks on the cliff face using the razor blade. Scraping out the colour in this way creates areas of light with hard edges (see page 20), giving form and definition to the cliff face.

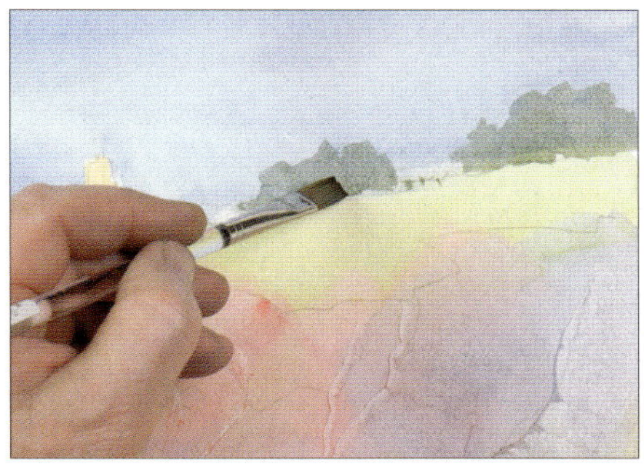

12 Mix together some cobalt blue and new gamboge and 'dab on' the trees at the top of the cliff using the smaller flat brush.

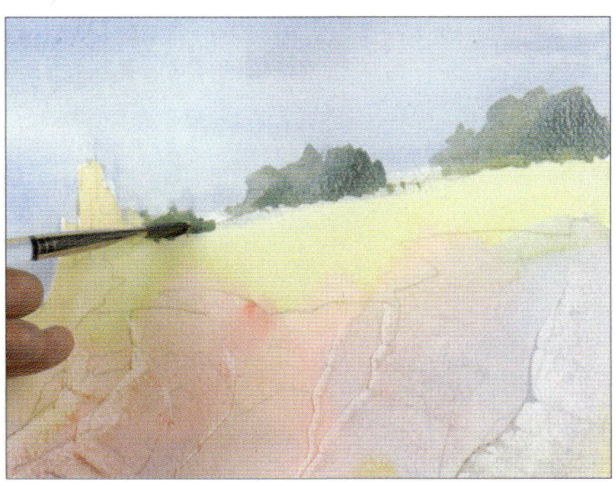

13 Make another mix with more blue and less yellow and put in the shadows on the right-hand sides of the trees.

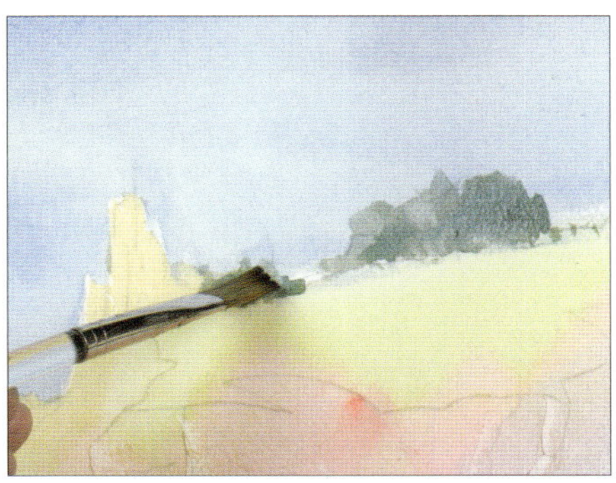

14 Clean the brush and use the corner of it to soften in the edges of the trees.

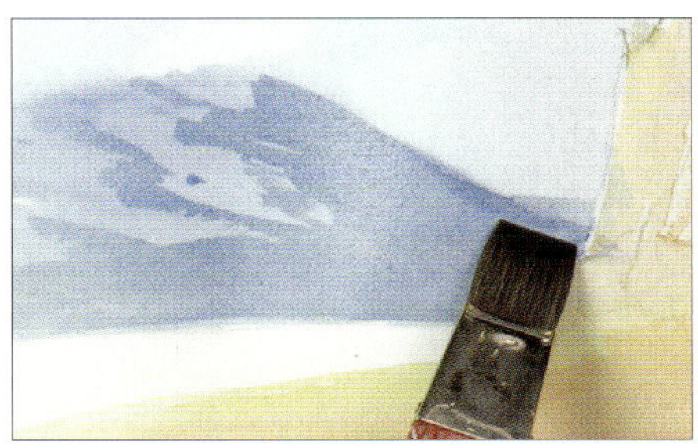

15 Using the standard shadow mix of cobalt blue, permanent rose and cadmium scarlet (see page 13) and the larger flat brush, paint on the shadows on the right-hand side of the distant mountain.

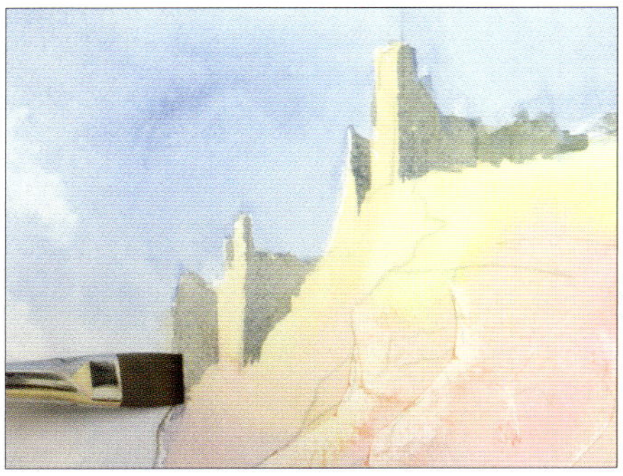

16 Change back to the smaller flat brush and put in the shadows on the sides of the castle facing away from the light. These are the form shadows. Use the flat edge of the brush.

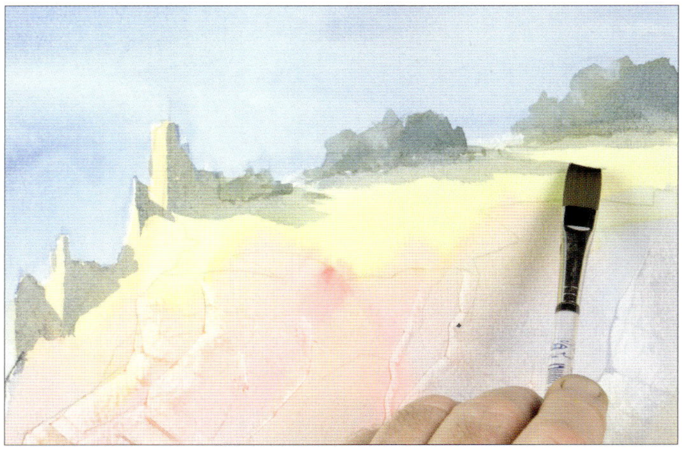

17 Use the same technique to put in the cast shadows sweeping away from the castle towards the right of the picture. Soften the edges of the shadows here and there using a clean, damp brush.

18 Put in the shadows on the cliff face to accentuate the light and help define the shapes of the rocks. Work your way across from left to right, linking the shadows in with the cast shadows at the top of the cliff on the left and with each other. Soften in the edges as you work.

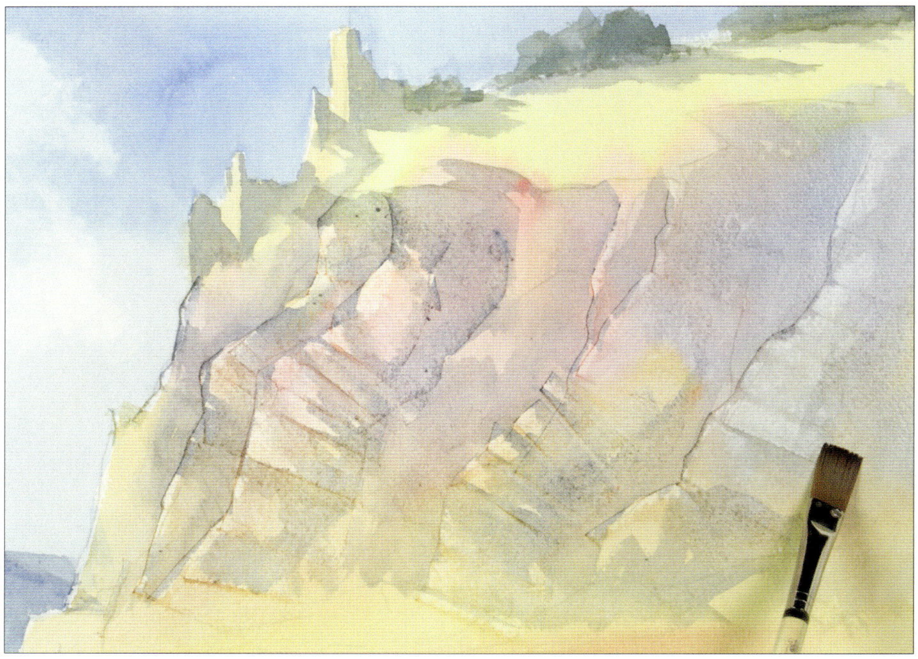

Tip

When using a razor blade to scrape out highlights, make sure the paint is still wet and place the razor blade with the edge flat on the surface. Tilt the blade in the direction you wish to scrape and push the pigment firmly in that direction. Be careful not to cut yourself.

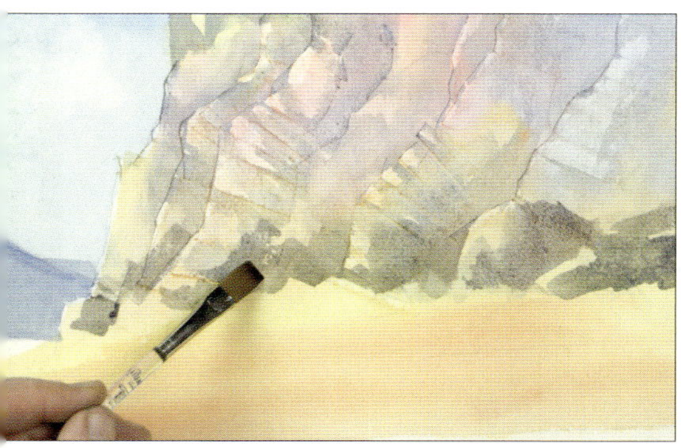

19 Mix together some cobalt blue and burnt sienna and put in the dark shadows on the rocks at the bottom of the cliff, leaving the light areas bare.

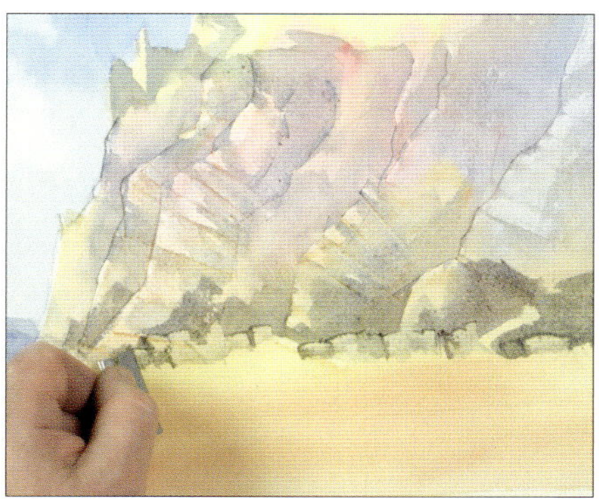

20 Use the razor blade to scrape out the smaller rocks at the front (see tip above). Soften the lower edge of the rocks using a clean, damp brush.

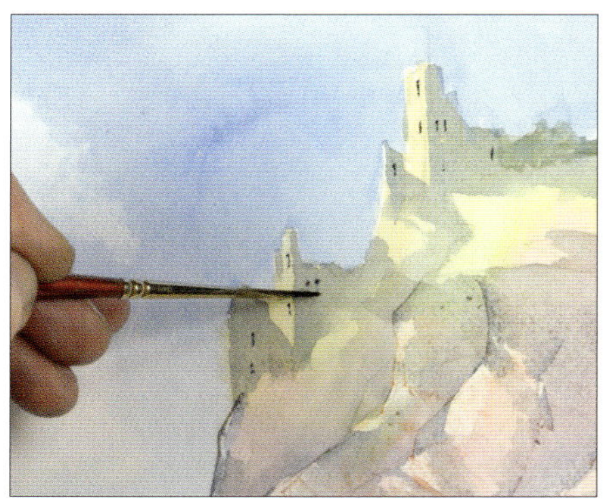

21 Make sure the castle is dry then put in the windows using the rigger and a dark mix of French ultramarine and burnt umber.

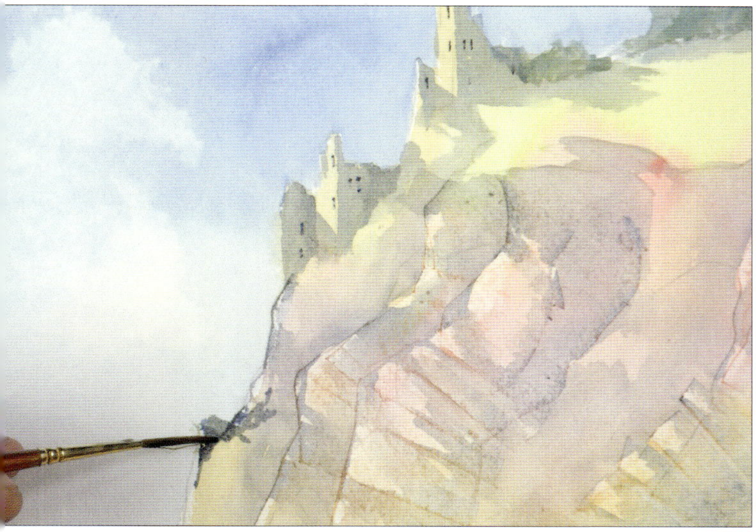

22 Using a mix of French ultramarine and cadmium scarlet, put more light into the castle by adding small patches of dark shadows behind it. Also deepen the rocky outcrop below it. Soften the edges.

Tip

Enhance the sunlit areas of your painting by deepening the shadows. Soften them in, but retain a hard edge where the lightest and darkest parts of the painting meet.

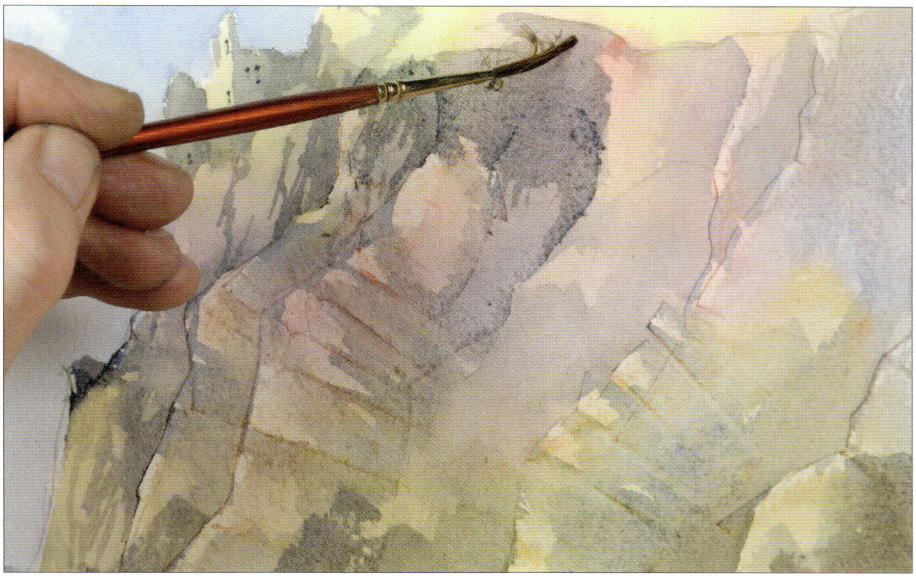

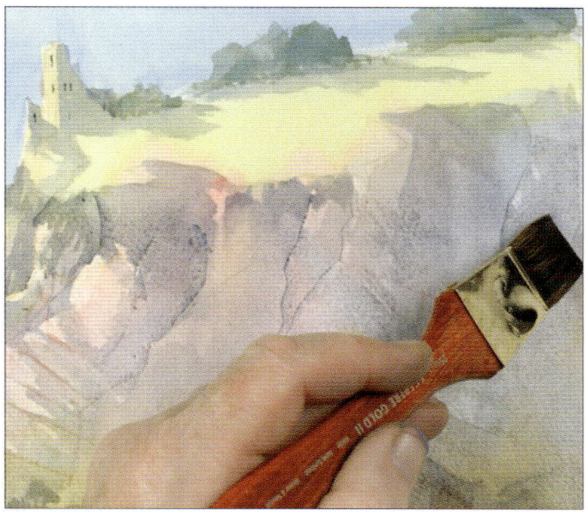

24 To avoid introducing too much detail, change to the large flat brush for the flatter areas on the right.

23 With the same mix, continue to deepen the darkest shadows on the cliff face. Use the rigger to work in more detail.

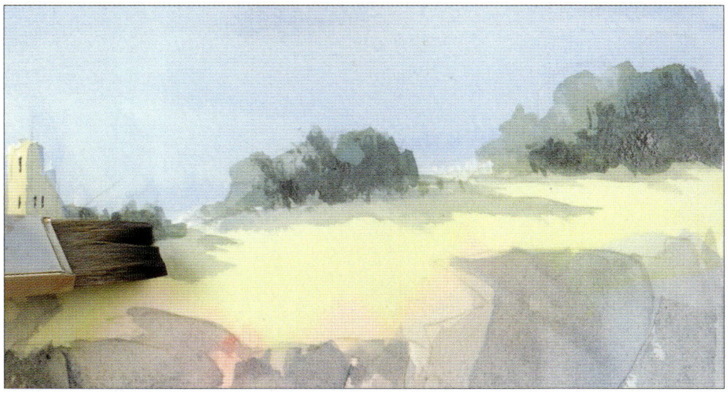

25 Using a mix of French ultramarine, new gamboge and cadmium scarlet, darken the right-hand sides of the trees. Apply the paint using the side of the brush for a 'sparkly' finish (see page 12).

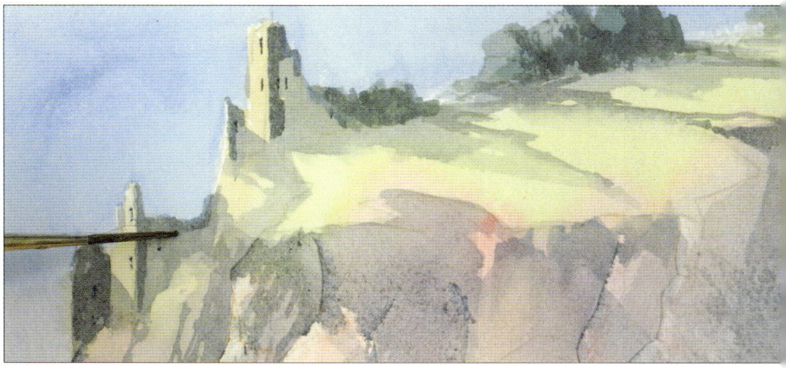

26 With the same mix, change to the rigger and extend the cast shadows on the top of the cliff. Also strengthen the shadows on the castle where they lie adjacent to the lightest areas and to the sky.

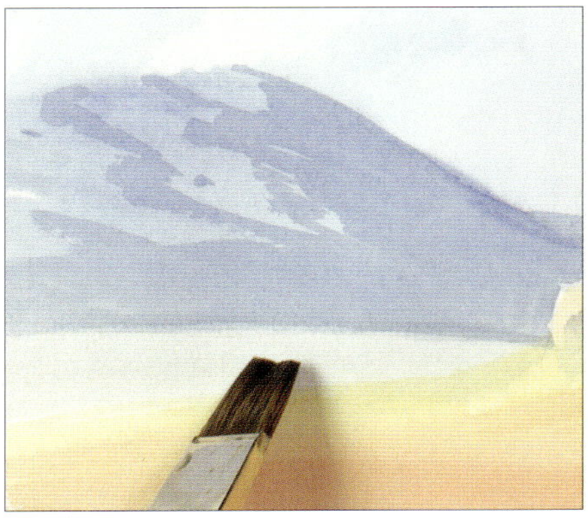

27 Use the large flat brush to dampen the area of water.

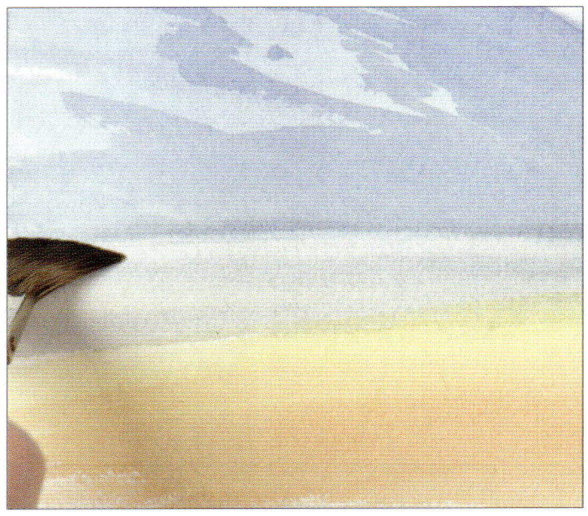

28 Put in the blue using a mix of French ultramarine and a little cadmium scarlet. Wring out the brush and define the water's edge by drawing along it with the flat edge of the brush.

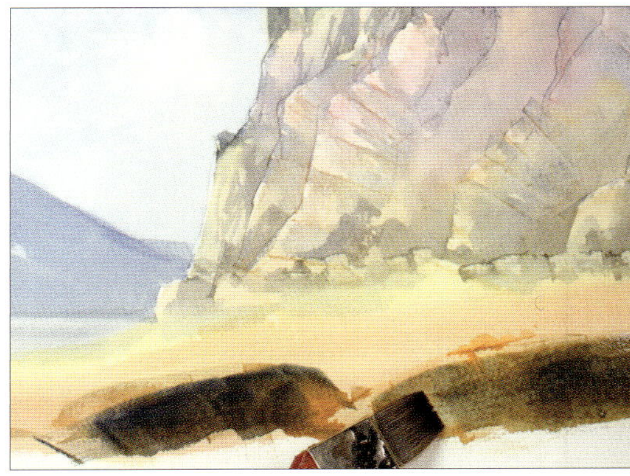

29 Put in the large foreground rocks using a wash of cadmium orange followed by French ultramarine.

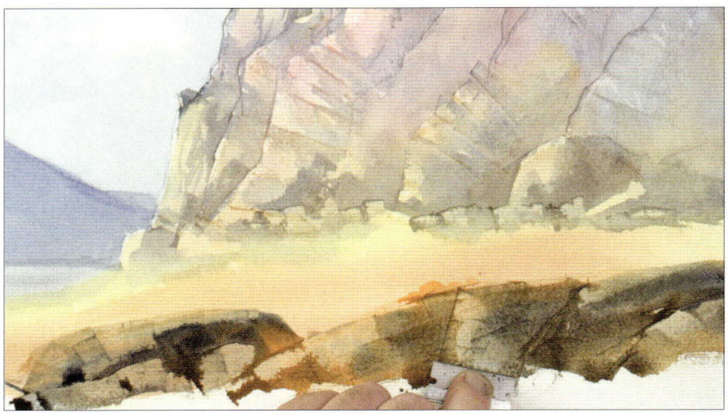

30 Scrape out the rocks, as you did in step 20.

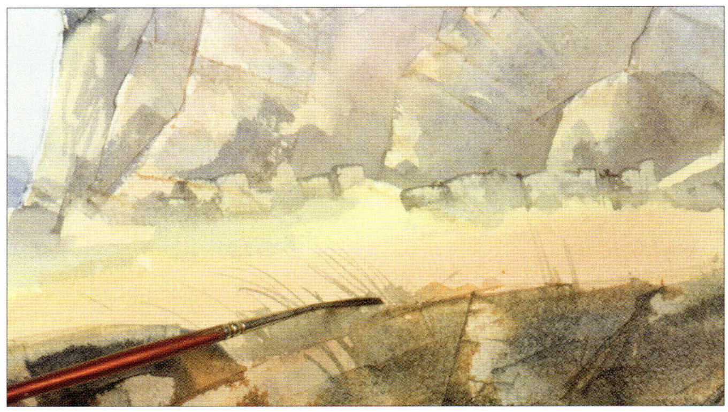

31 Make a mix of new gamboge and cobalt blue and, holding the rigger right at the end, paint in some grasses using swift, curving strokes of the brush.

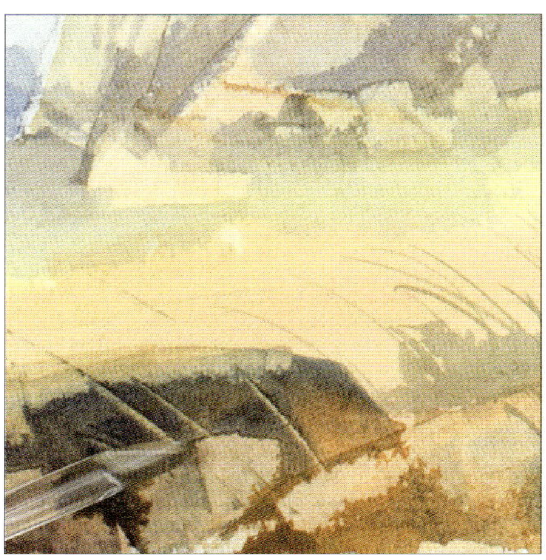

32 For the lighter-coloured grasses, use the same movement, but scrape them out with the scraper end of the 13mm (½in) flat brush.

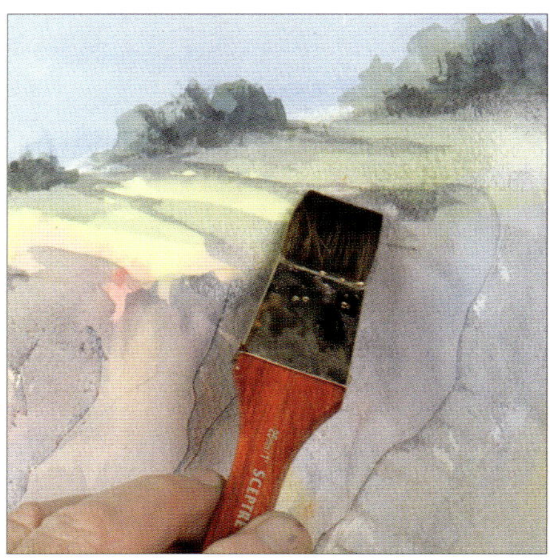

33 Using the larger flat brush, put more shadows on the right-hand side of the picture to draw the eye towards the castle.

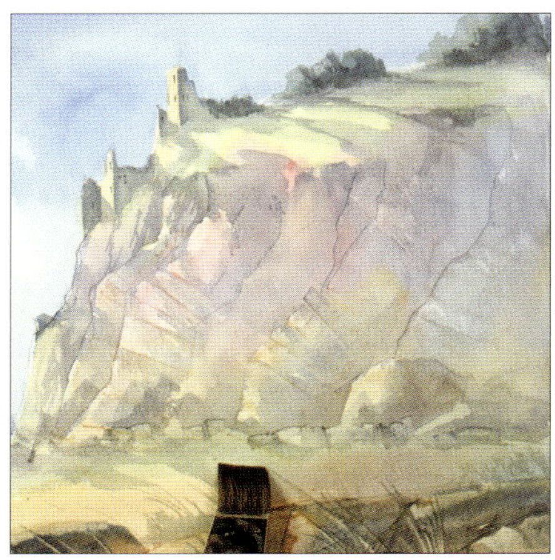

34 Also bring in more shadow at the foot of the cliff to force the eye into the centre of the painting.

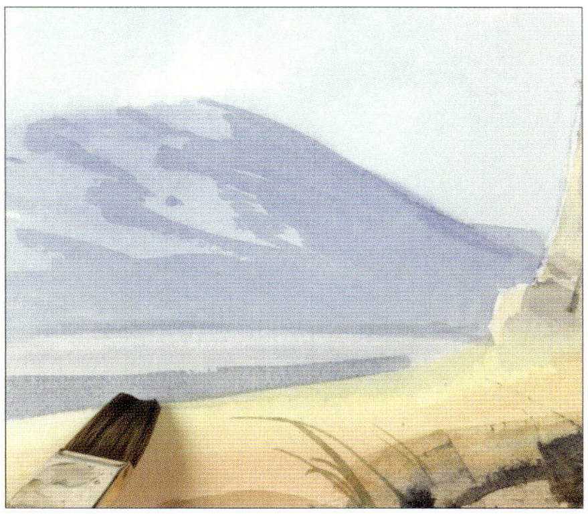

35 Darken the lower part of the water using cobalt blue and cadmium scarlet to enhance the suggestion of sunlight at the edge of the lake.

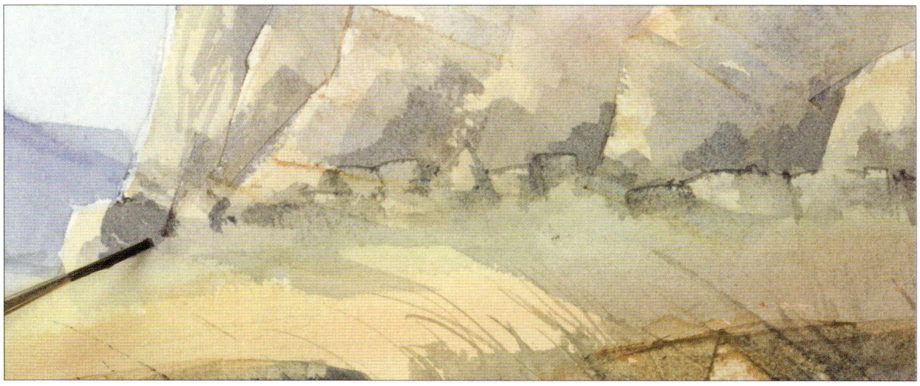

36 Change to the rigger, and put more sunlight on to the rocks at the foot of the cliff by deepening the shadows on their right-hand sides.

Tip

Remember to soften in the colour as you paint to avoid hard edges and give a more natural finish to your painting.

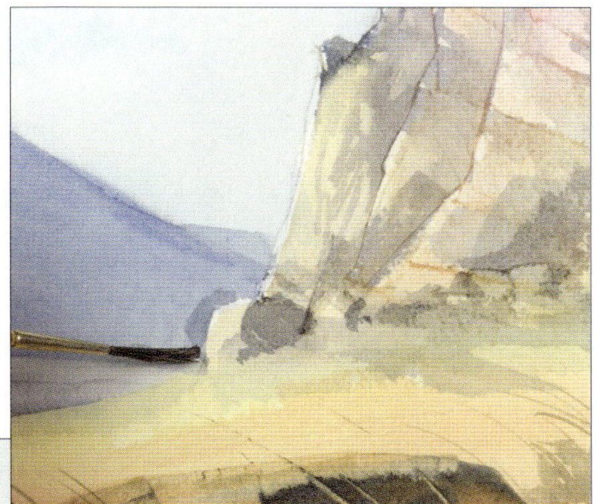

37 Also darken the corner of the lake adjacent to the cliff to accentuate the sunlight falling on to the rock furthest to the left.

Tip

Complete your painting by removing any visible pencil lines when it is completely dry.

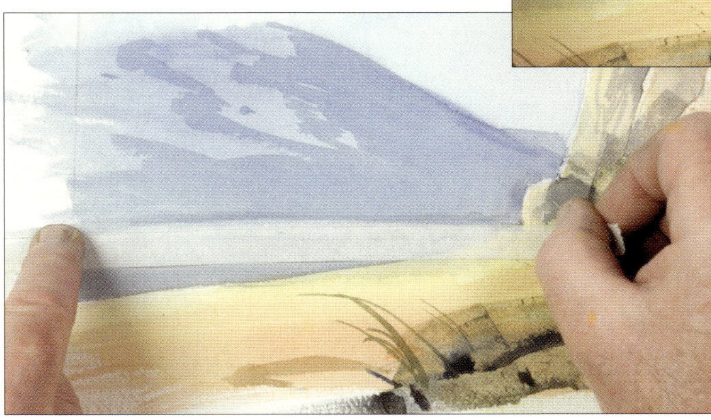

38 If necessary, straighten the edge of the lake by laying the top edge of a piece of masking tape along it and pressing it down firmly on to the paper. (Make sure the paint is completely dry before you do this.)

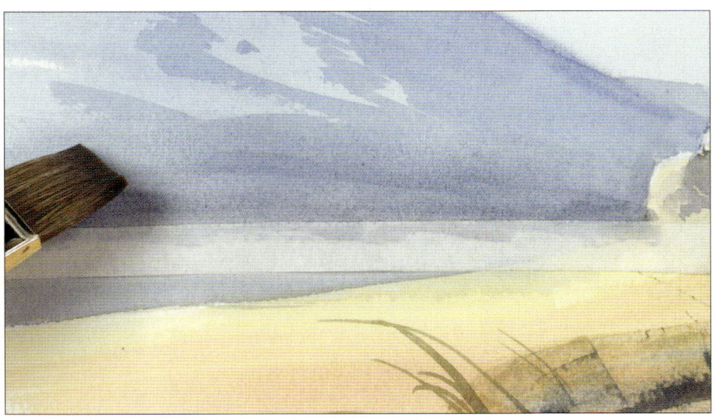

39 Using the same mix as you used in step 28, apply the paint by brushing from the top edge of the tape on to the paper. Soften the edge with clean water.

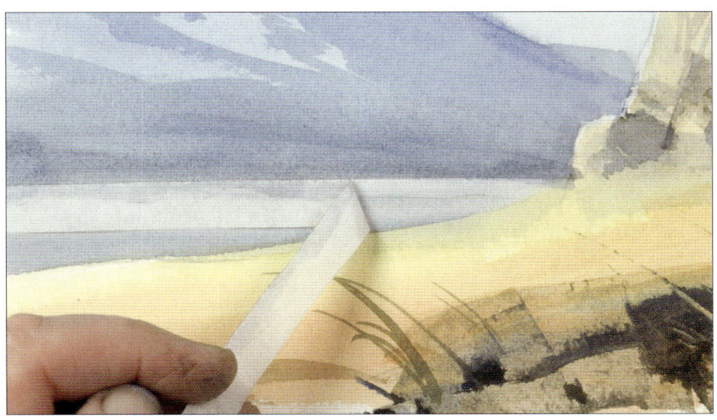

40 When the paint is dry, pull the masking tape away from the painting.

Overleaf

The finished painting.

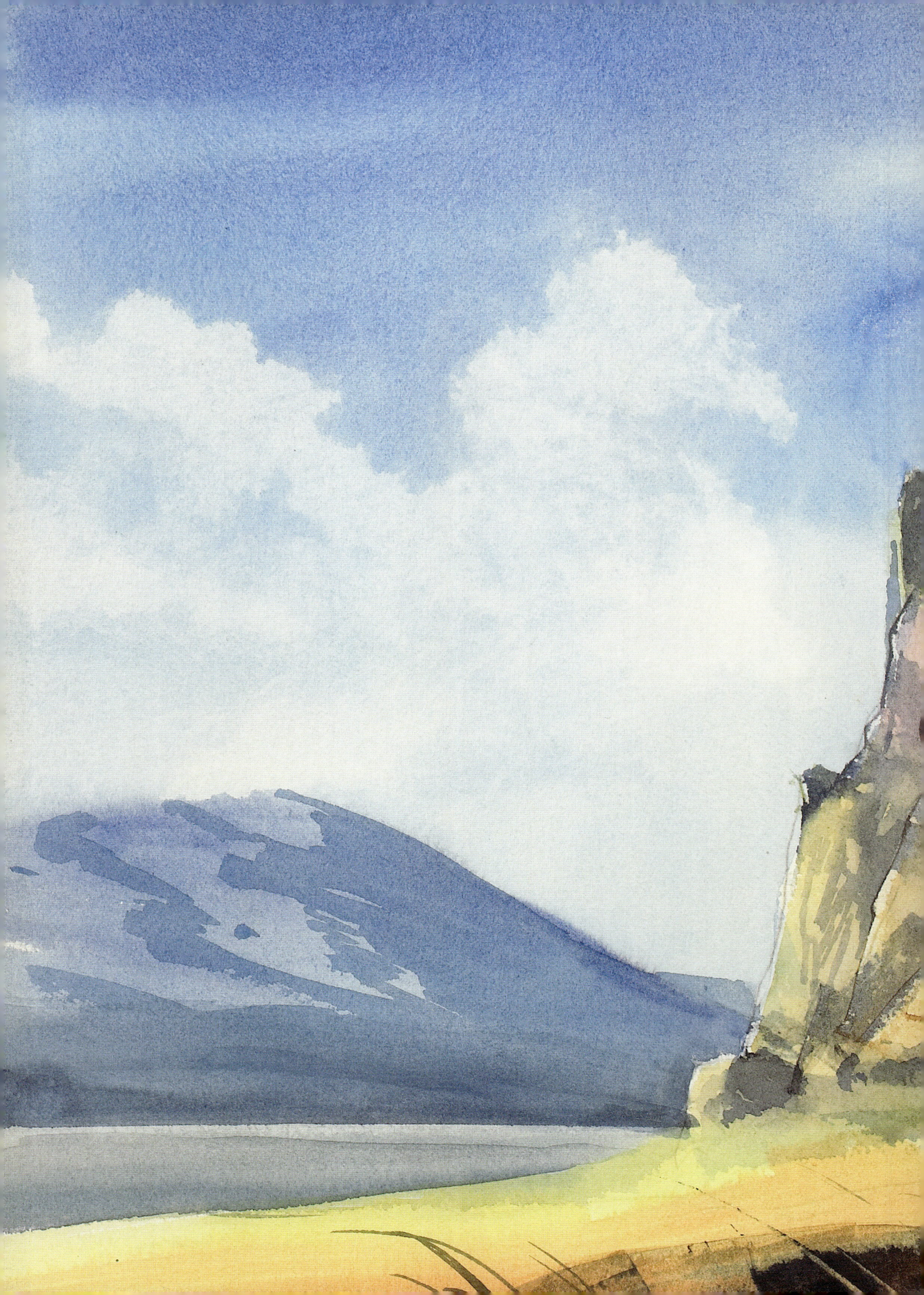

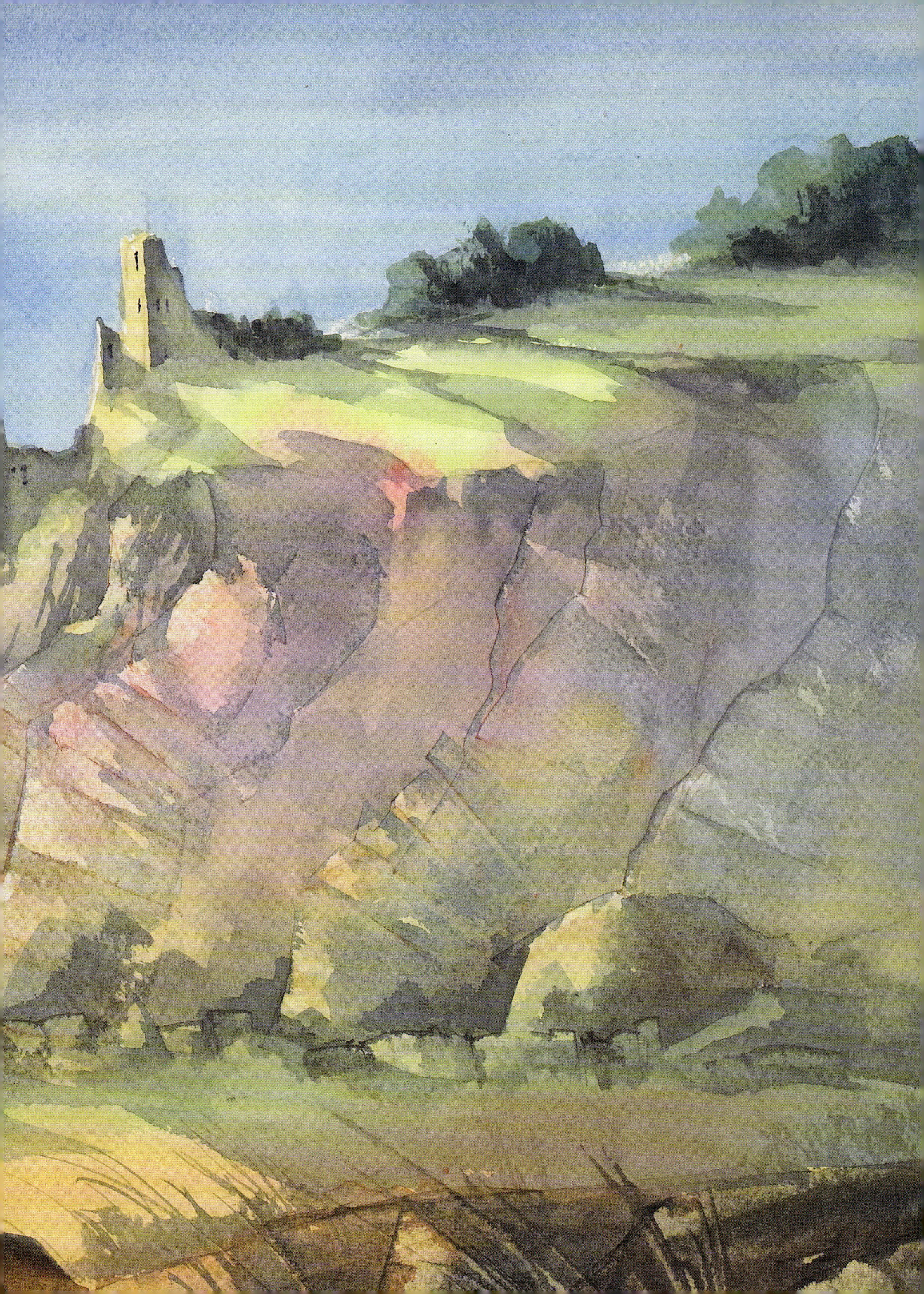

Mountain Stream

TRACING 6

I wanted to emphasise the gentleness of the rolling hills in the distance in this painting, so I placed a waterfall in the foreground to act as a foil. For variety I added a ploughed field. The foreground water and the sky are soft and calm, which helps to force the eye to the central area of the painting, which is where I want the viewer to look.

You will need

180gsm (90lb) NOT watercolour paper

Kneadable (putty) eraser

Safety razor blade

Kitchen paper

Small piece of sponge

Brushes: 25mm (1in) flat brush; 13mm (½in) flat brush with a scraper end; no. 3 rigger

Paints: cadmium scarlet, cobalt blue, French ultramarine, cadmium lemon, new gamboge, Winsor blue (green shade), cadmium orange, burnt sienna, burnt umber, permanent rose and titanium white

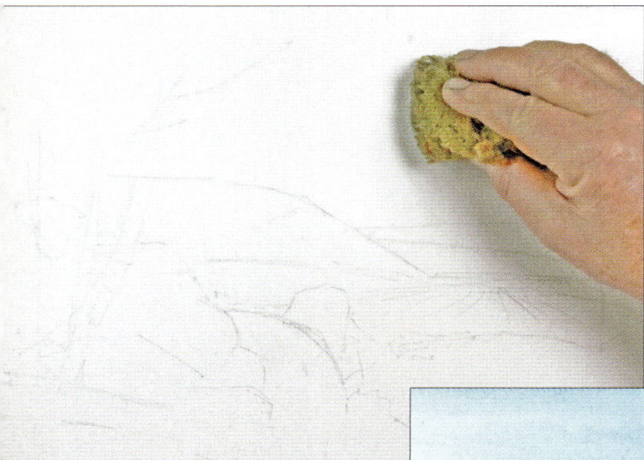

1 Begin by dampening the sky using a damp sponge. Avoid over-wetting the paper.

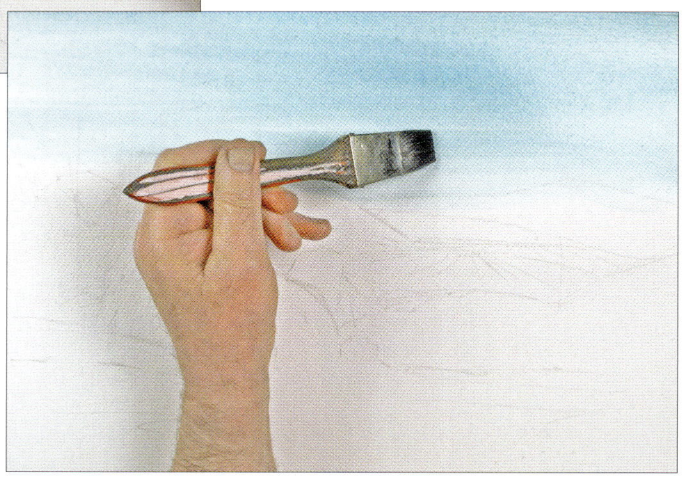

2 Before it dries, make a thin mix of Winsor blue (green shade) and a tiny amount of cadmium scarlet and paint in the sky, taking the colour down over the tops of the mountains. Use the 25mm (1in) flat brush.

3 Dab out a suggestion of clouds using a crumpled piece of dry kitchen paper.

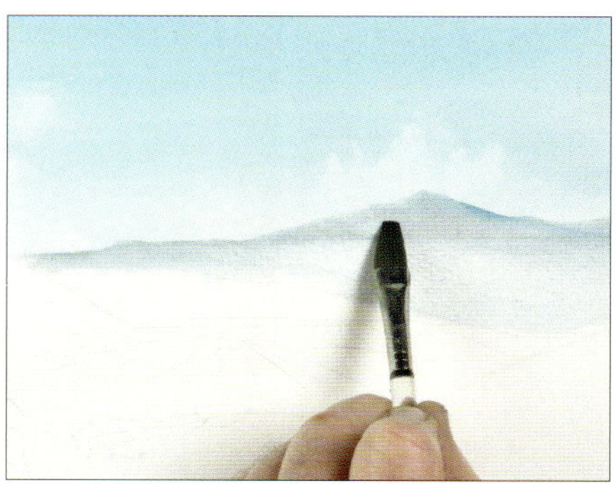

4 Add a little cadmium scarlet to the mix and put in the tops of the distant mountains using the smaller flat brush. Fade the colour out towards the bottom.

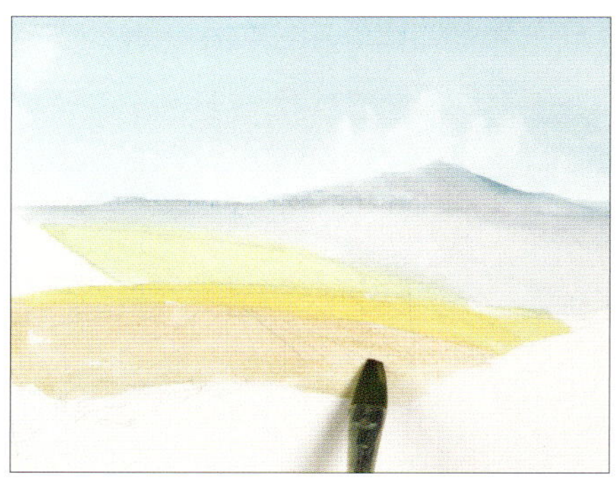

5 Use a little cadmium lemon to put in the hill in the mid-ground. Moving forwards towards the foreground, put in the next hill using new gamboge, and the one in front of that using burnt sienna.

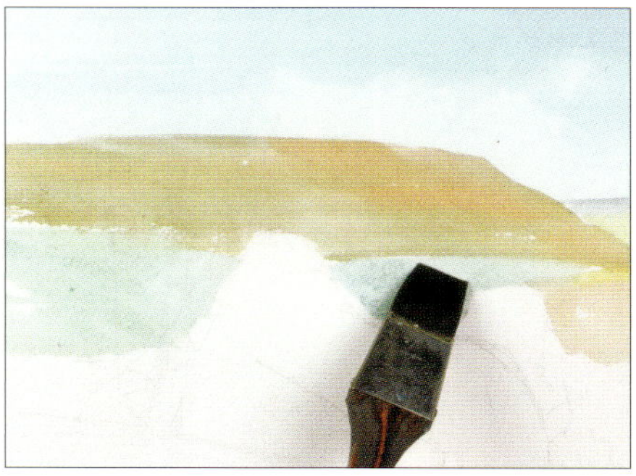

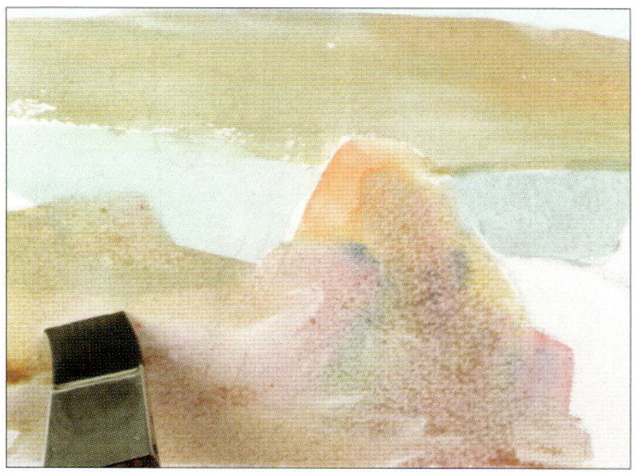

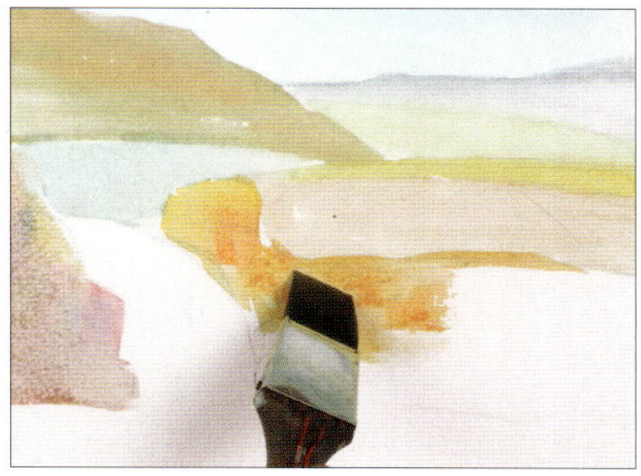

6 For the hill on the left, use more autumnal colours – new gamboge, cadmium scarlet and a little cobalt blue. Apply the paint with the larger flat brush. Paint the area in front of the hill using a mix of Winsor blue (green shade) and a little cadmium lemon.

7 Begin to put in the rocks in the foreground. Use new gamboge, a little cadmium orange and some cadmium scarlet, a touch of cobalt blue and some permanent rose. Lay the colours in separately and allow them to mix on the paper.

8 For the rocks in the middle of the picture use cadmium orange, new gamboge and some cadmium scarlet.

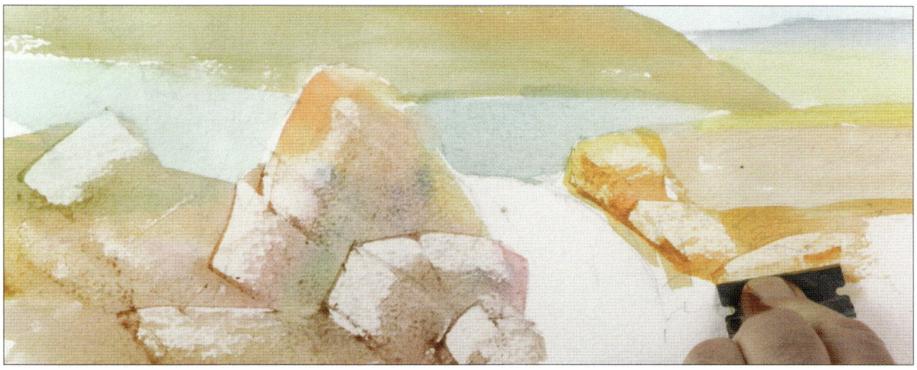

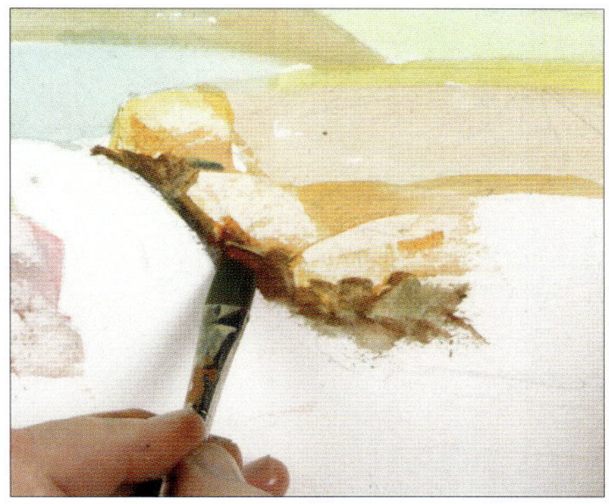

9 Use a razor blade to scrape away the paint where the sunlight catches the rocks. This adds depth and texture. (The light is coming from the left.)

10 Using the small flat brush, put in some dark foliage and strengthen the edge of the waterfall. Use Winsor blue (green shade) and burnt umber.

Tip

When using a razor blade to scrape out highlights, make sure the paint is still wet and place the razor blade with the edge flat on the surface. Tilt the blade in the direction you wish to scrape and firmly push the pigment in that direction.

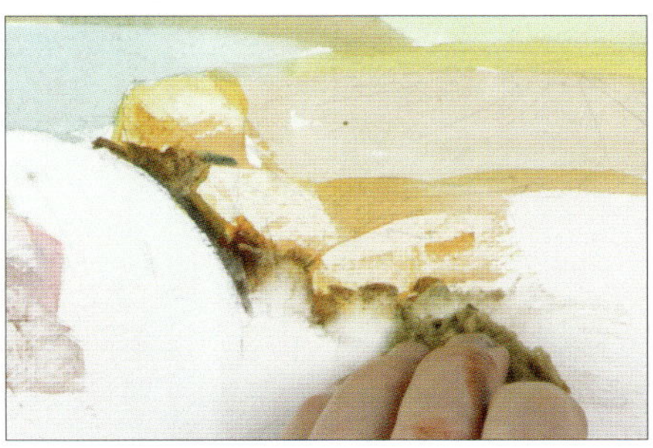

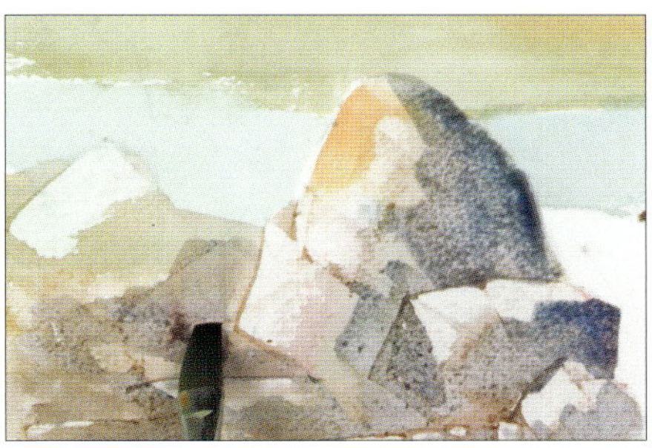

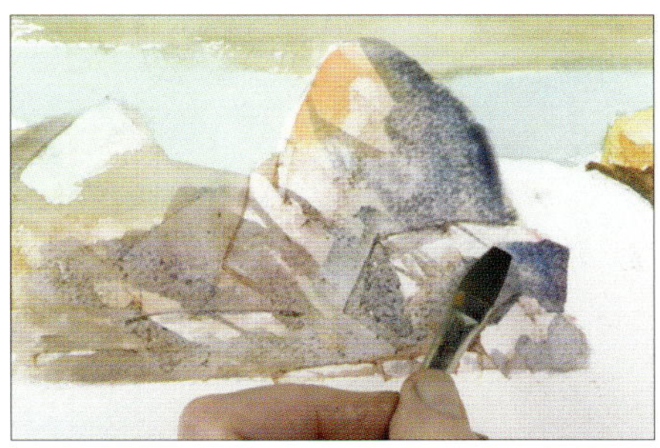

11 Work into the paint firmly with a damp sponge, pushing the pigment to one side. This creates soft patches of white, which will eventually become areas of spray rising from the waterfall.

12 Make up a small quantity of shadow mix (see page 18) and put in the shadows on the left-hand rocks.

13 Put in the diagonal shadows cast by the trees. Soften the base of the rocks with a damp sponge if necessary.

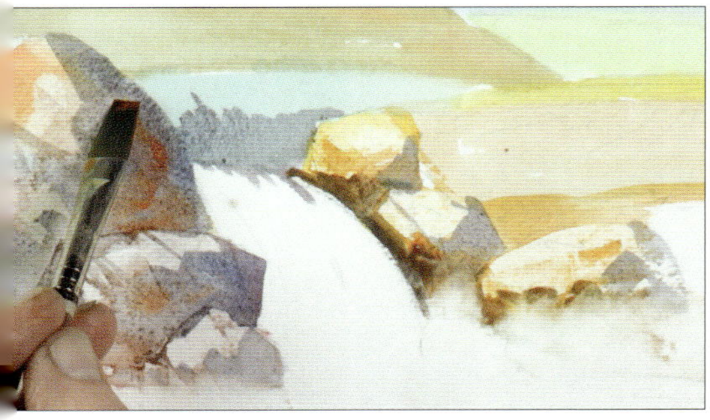

14 Add shadows to the rocks on the right, and use the same mix to put in the suggestion of distant foliage at the top of the waterfall. Introduce more cadmium orange into the foreground rocks on the left.

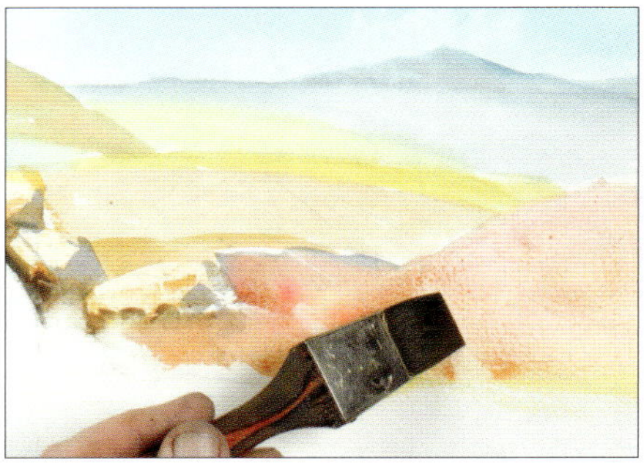

15 Paint the area of foreground on the right of the picture using a mixture of yellows, blues, reds and oranges. Apply them singly and allow them to blend on the paper.

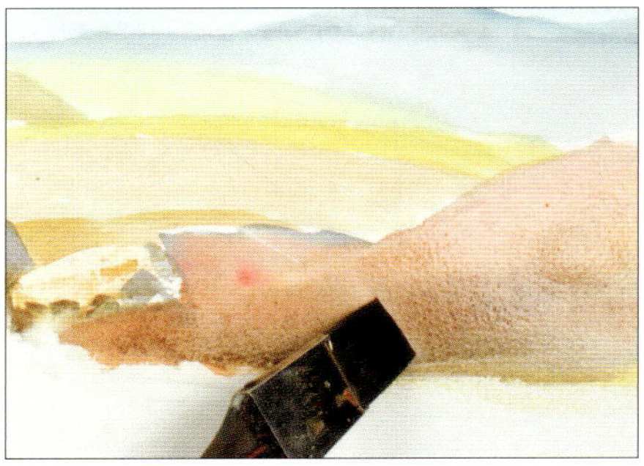

16 Darken the lower area using burnt sienna and French ultramarine.

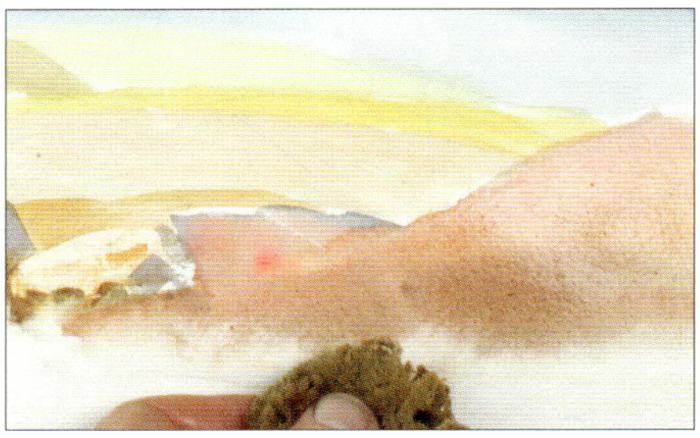

17 Push a damp sponge up into the lower edge of the paint to suggest foam at the base of the waterfall.

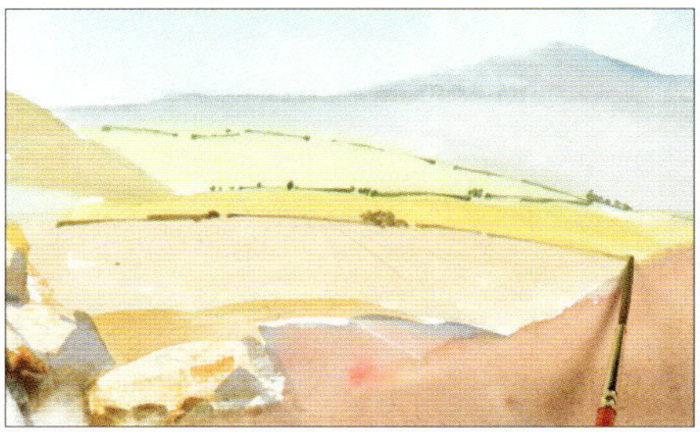

18 Using the no. 3 rigger, put in the distant hedgerows as thin, irregular, broken lines with occasional dots of paint for trees and shrubs. For those in the distance use a mix of new gamboge and cobalt blue; for those further forwards add a little more red.

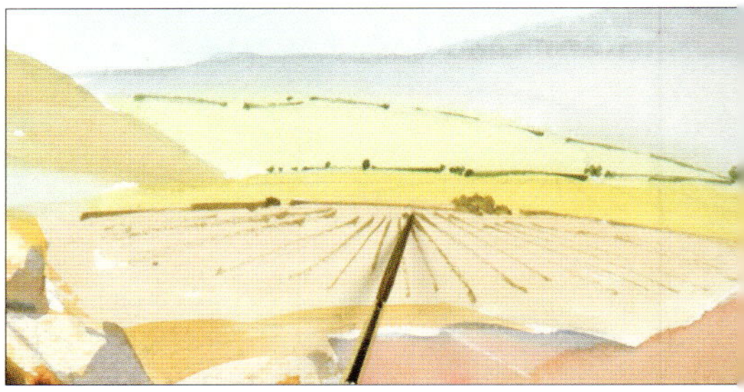

19 With the more red version of the mix, draw in the thin, radiating lines denoting the furrows of the ploughed field.

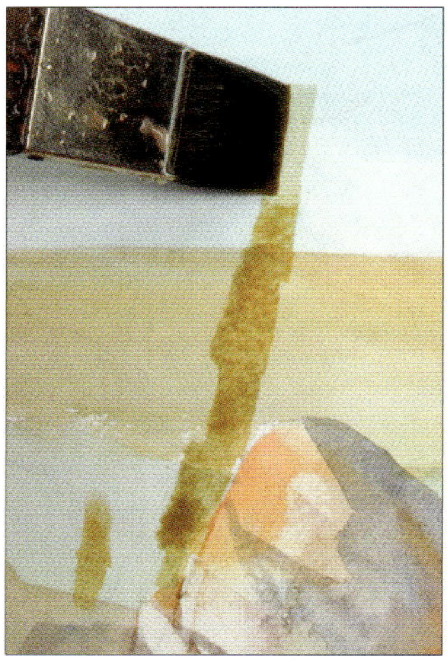

20 Start to place the main trees on the left. Use the larger flat brush and the same green mix as in the previous step. Apply the paint with the flat edge of the brush and using horizontal strokes, pulling the paint from one side of the trunk to the other.

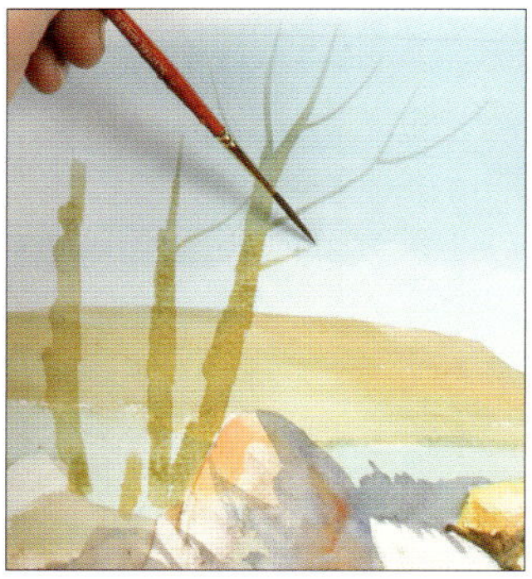

21 Returning to the rigger, put in three trunks, all at slightly different angles, then add a little more blue to the mix and put in the main branches at the tops of the trees. Paint each branch with a single, sweeping stroke from the trunk to its tip.

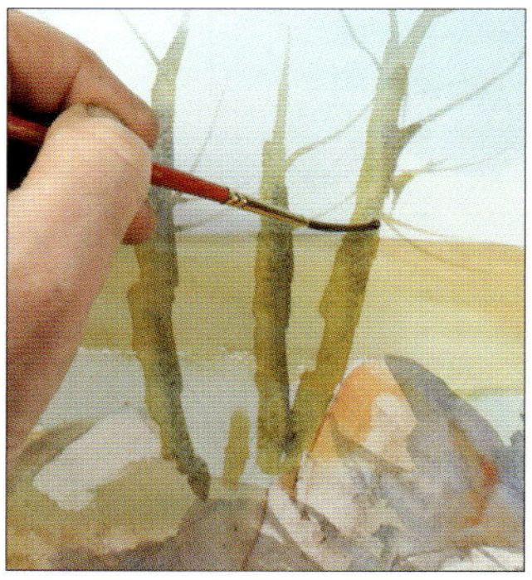

22 Use the shadow mix (see step 12) to lay in the shadows down the right-hand sides of the tree trunks (the light is coming from the left).

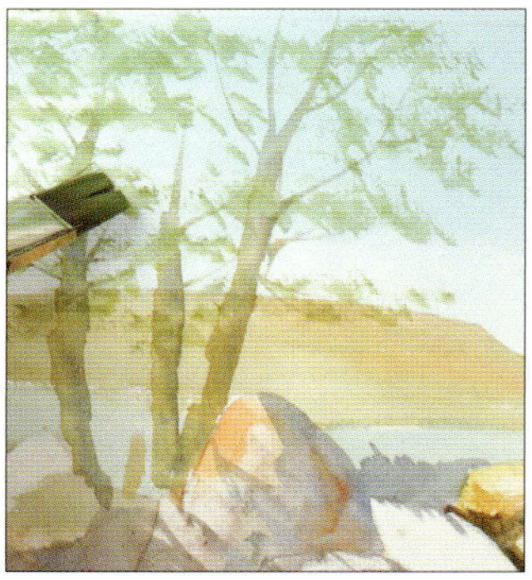

23 For the foliage, make a mix of cobalt blue, cadmium lemon and a touch of cadmium orange. Dab the paint on firmly using the corner of the 25mm (1in) flat brush – this will give your painting a more 'sparkly' finish (see page 12).

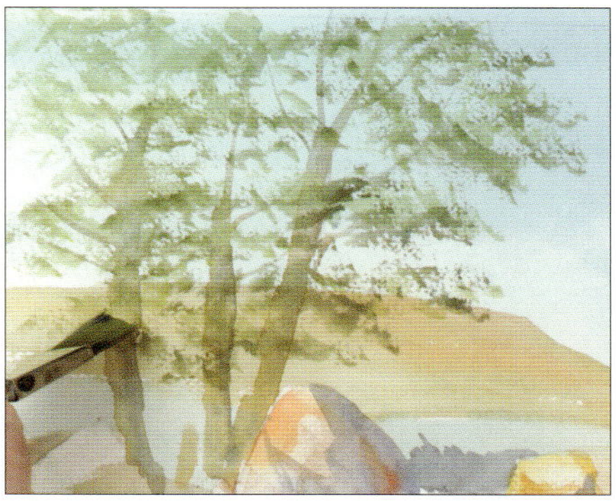

24 Add a little red to the mix for the darker foliage at the bottom and on the right.

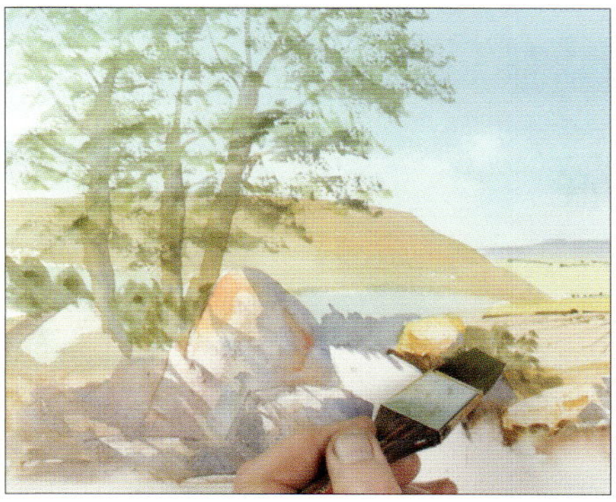

25 Use the darker green to put in some shrubs at the base of the trees and on the right-hand side of the waterfall.

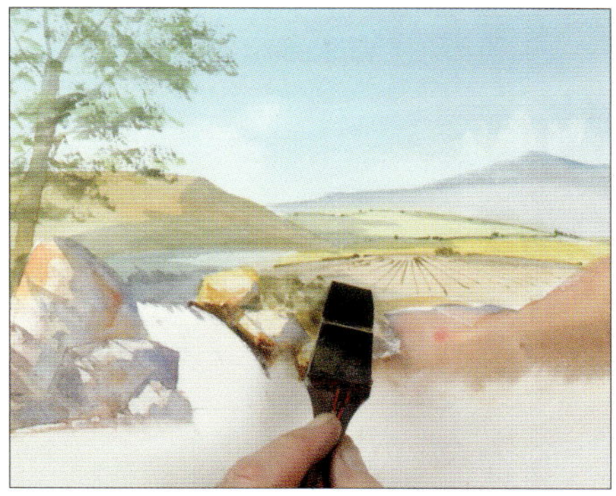

26 With the standard shadow mix (see step 12), use the flat edge of the brush to place the shadows on the right-facing side of the mid-ground mountains and across the fields in the background.

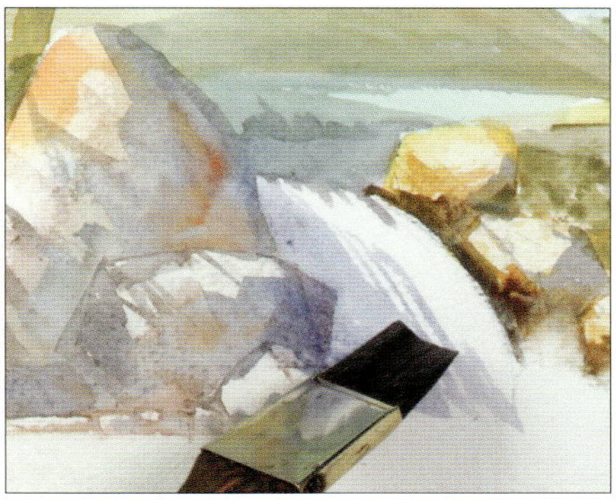

27 Use the corner of the brush to paint on the shadows on the waterfall, in the same direction as the flow of the water.

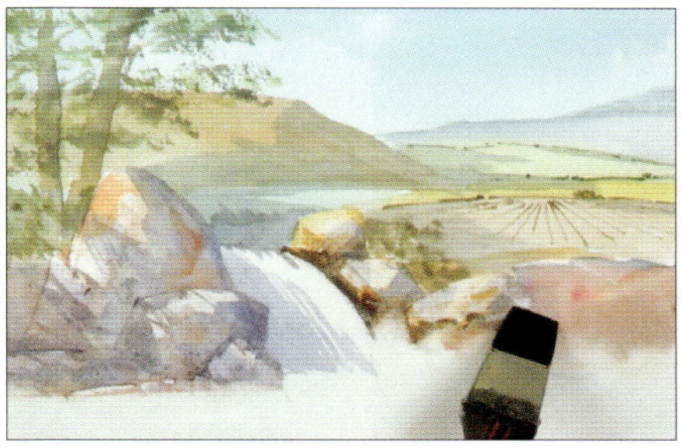

28 Strengthen the shadows on the rocks on the left and on the area of ground on the right.

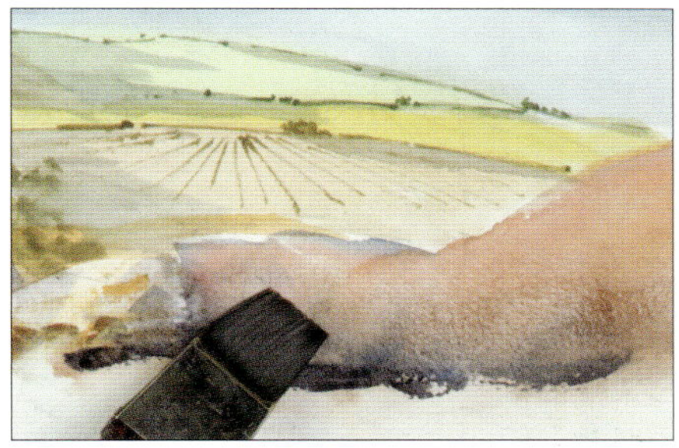

29 Make a dark mix of burnt sienna and French ultramarine and put in the darks at the base of the ground to the right of the waterfall. Soften the edges with a clean, damp brush.

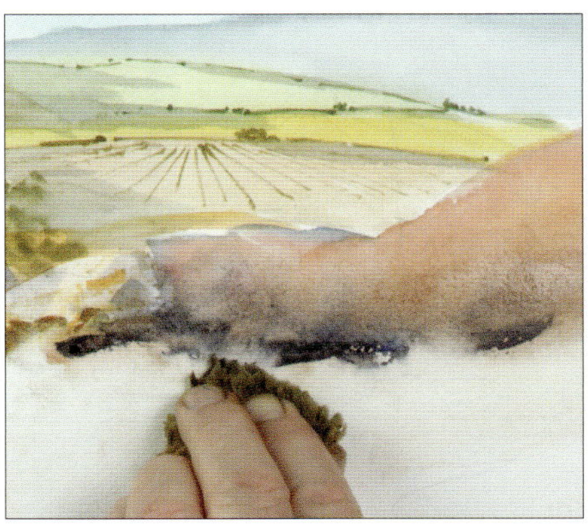

30 Use a damp sponge to soften the bottom edge here and there, where it meets the edge of the water.

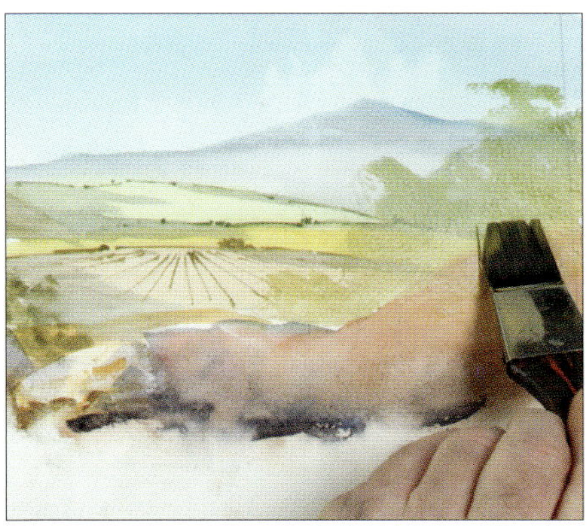

31 Put in the shrubs and bushes on the right using the light green mix used for the foliage in step 23 (cobalt blue, cadmium lemon and a touch of cadmium orange).

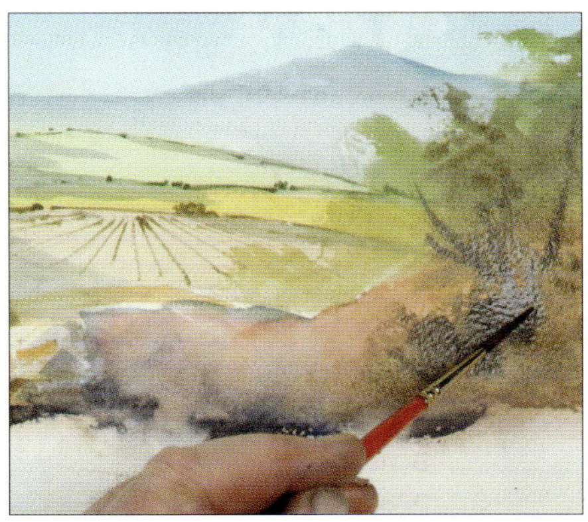

32 Strengthen the colour with the darker green, then paint in some branches using the burnt sienna and French ultramarine mix and the no. 3 rigger.

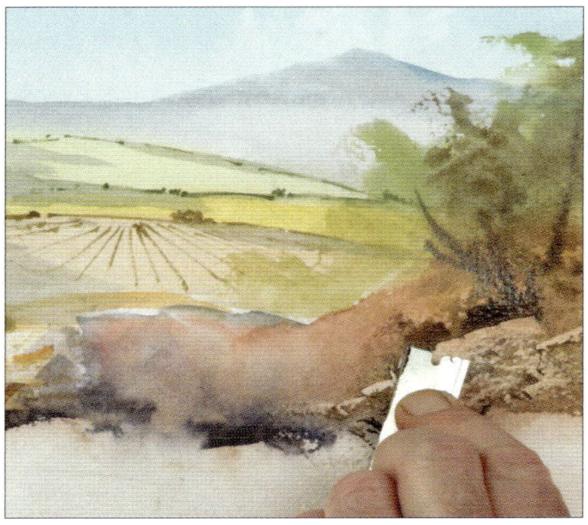

33 Scrape out the rocks below the shrubs using the razor blade, as you did in step 9.

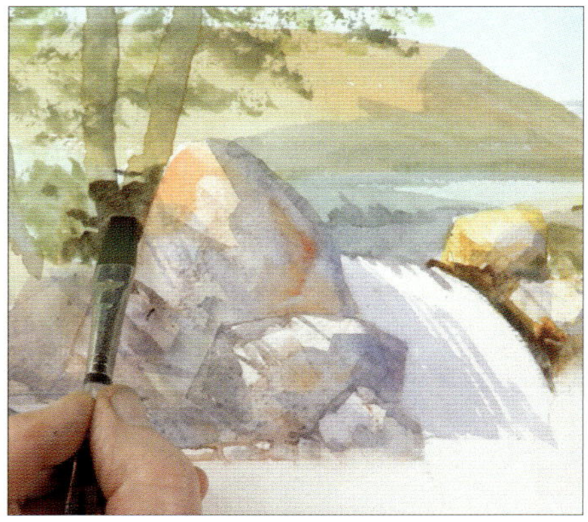

34 Using a very dark green mix of cadmium lemon, French ultramarine and cadmium scarlet, darken the foliage at the base of the large trees on the left. This will make the light areas look lighter. Use the smaller flat brush.

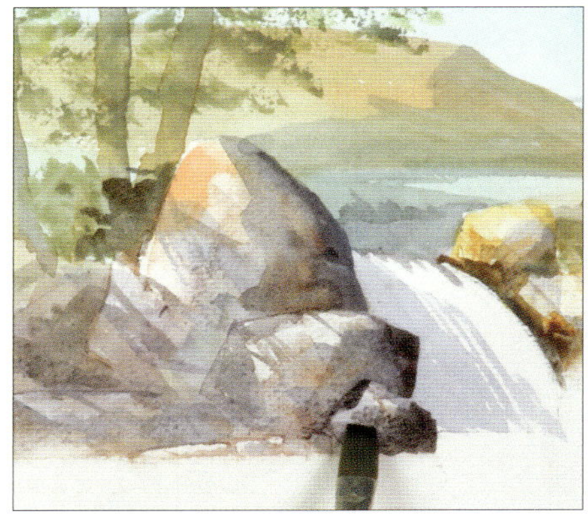

35 Make a cooler version of the mix by adding some cobalt blue and place a strong shadow down the right-hand side of the main rocks. Soften it in with a clean, damp brush.

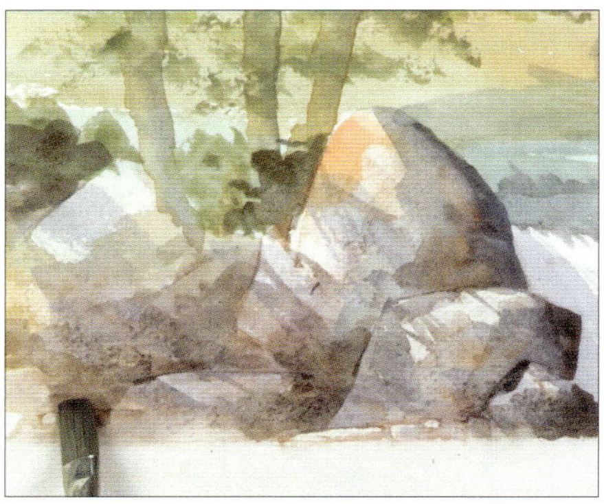

36 Using a slightly weaker version of the same mix, place more shadows on the remainder of the rocks. Soften them in as before.

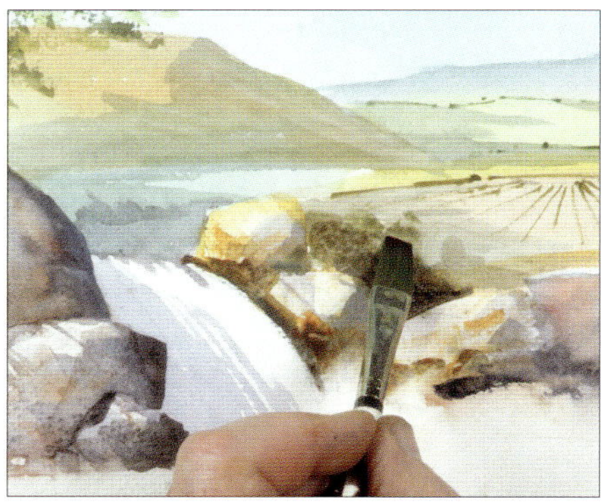

37 Apply shadows to the right-hand rocks in the same way.

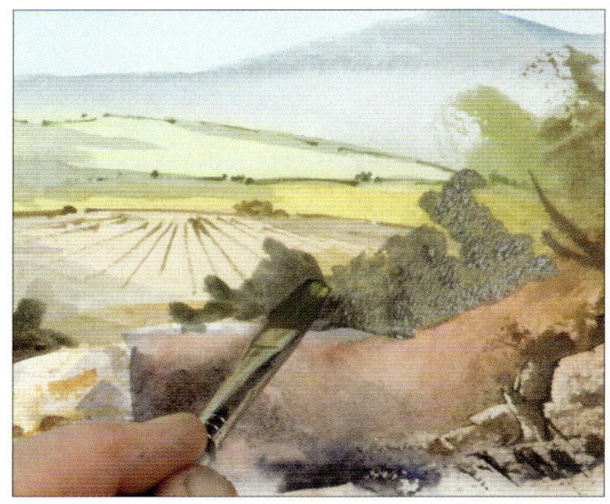

38 Deepen the colour of the shrubs and bushes on the right-hand side of the picture using the same dark green mix as the one you used in step 34.

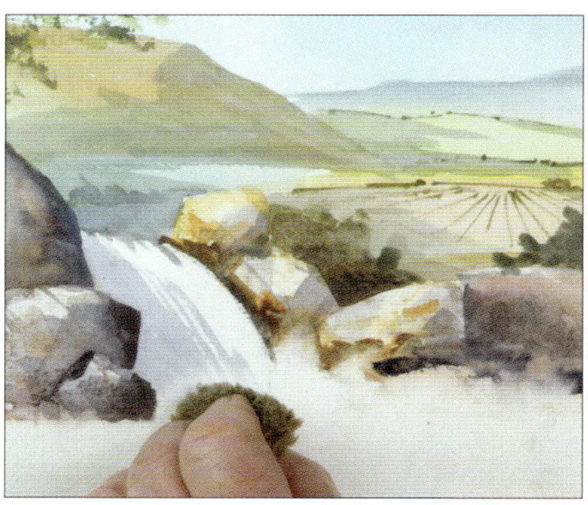

39 Soften the edges of the waterfall using a damp sponge, if these have started to dry.

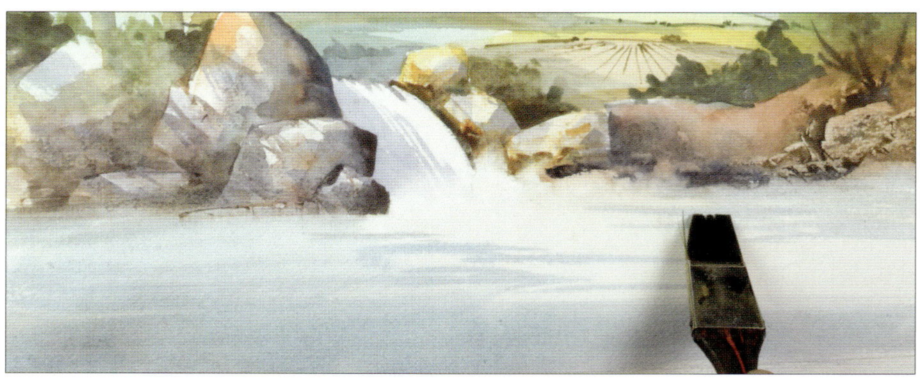

40 Dampen the area of water with a clean, damp sponge, then paint it using a pale mix of cobalt blue (the same colour as that used for the sky). Apply the paint using horizontal strokes of the larger flat brush. Create ripples by moving the edge of the brush horizontally across the wet paint. Ensure there is less water in the brush than on the paper – the water will then be drawn from the paper to the brush. Leave the area in front of the waterfall free of colour.

Tip

To create sparkle on the water, hold the brush flat against the surface and drag it across without pushing the paint into the paper.

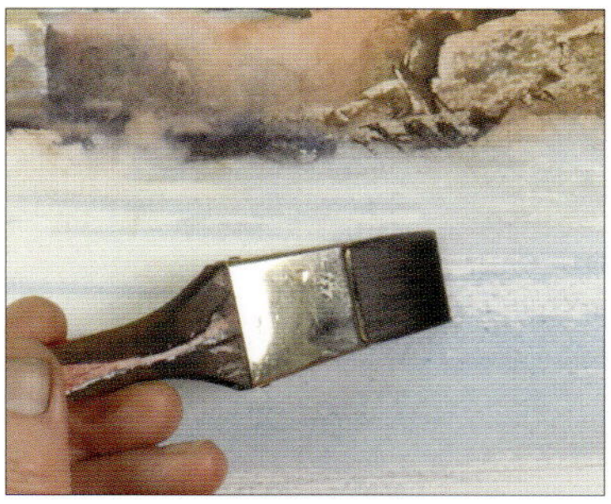

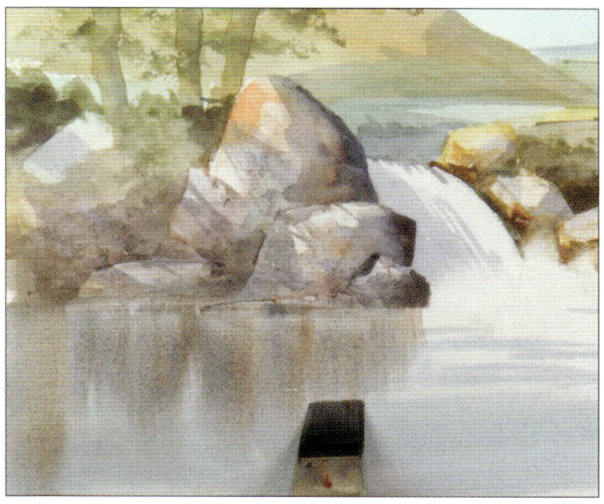

41 Using the same variety of colours you used for the rocks, drag the reflections from the base of the rocks into the water. Try to keep the tonal values the same.

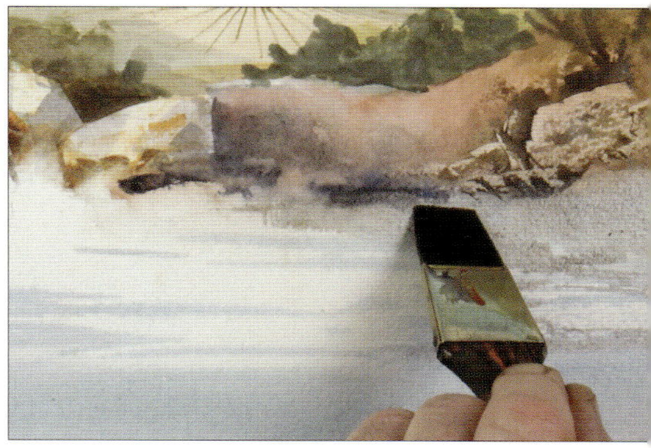

42 Do the same on the other side of the picture.

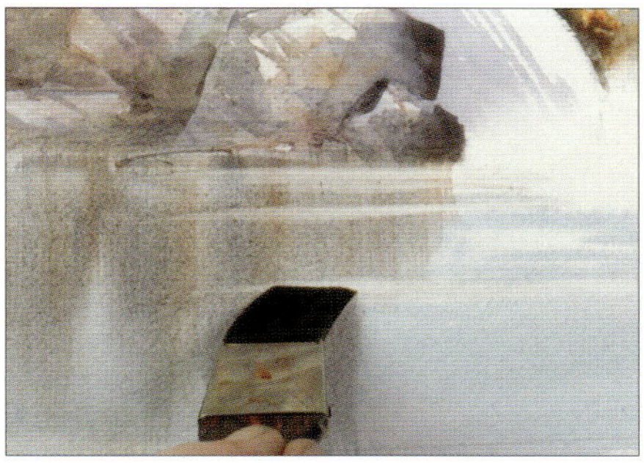

43 Clean the brush thoroughly and extend the ripples into the reflections using the technique described in step 40.

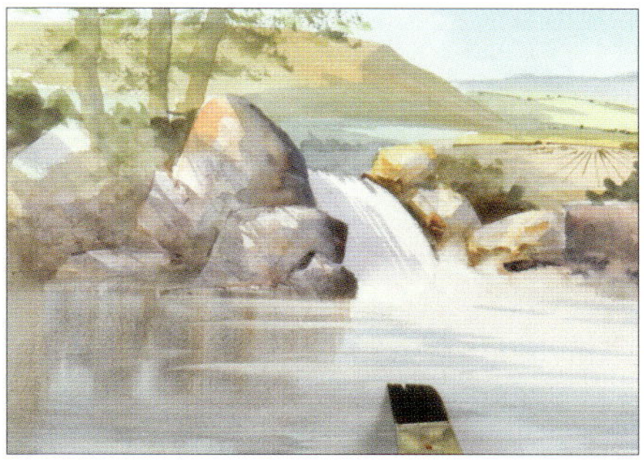

44 Pull some of the darks into the middle part of the water.

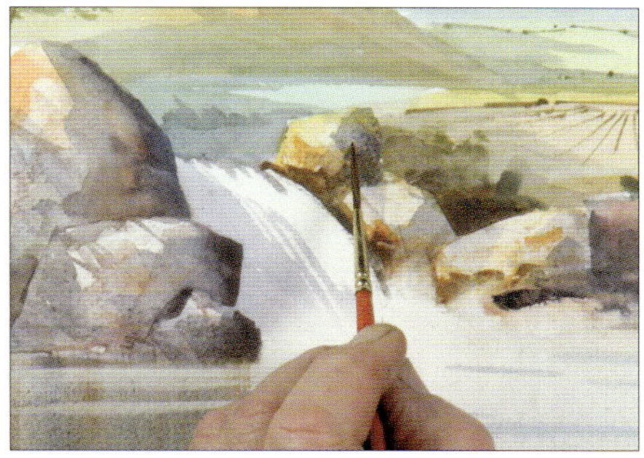

45 Add more shadows to the rocks where necessary to make them stand out against the background. Use the no. 3 rigger.

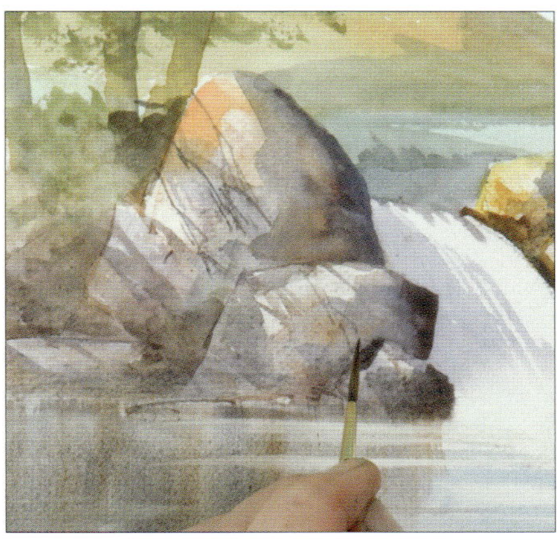

46 Using a very dark brown mix of French ultramarine and cadmium scarlet paint in the cracks on the left-hand rocks.

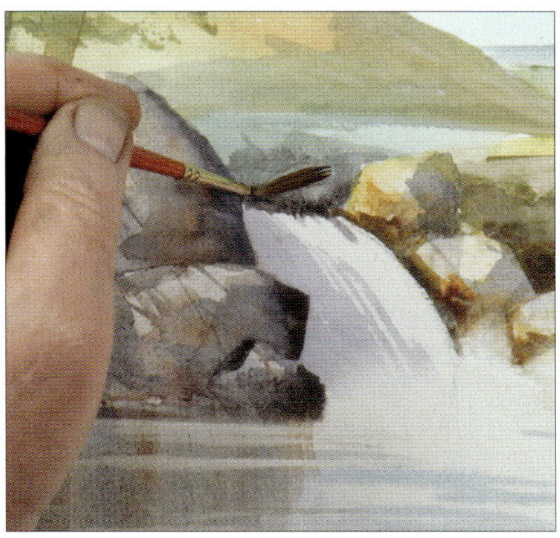

47 Put more of this mix behind the waterfall at the top to make the waterfall appear brighter. Soften it in with a clean, damp brush.

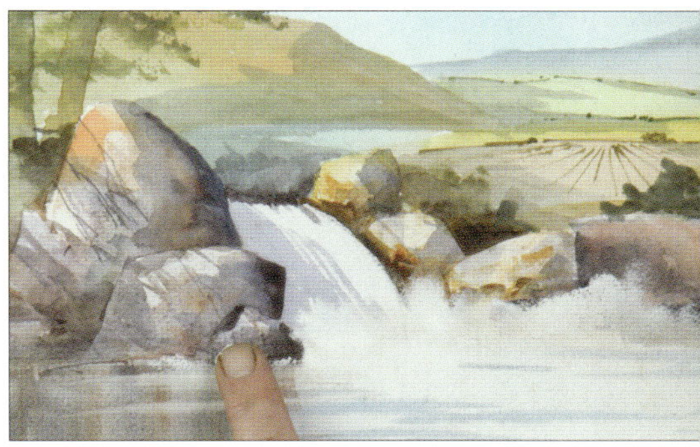

48 To create foam, use your finger to roll some undiluted titanium white into the bottom of the waterfall where it hits the water and the rocks. Do the same at the base of the rocks on the left.

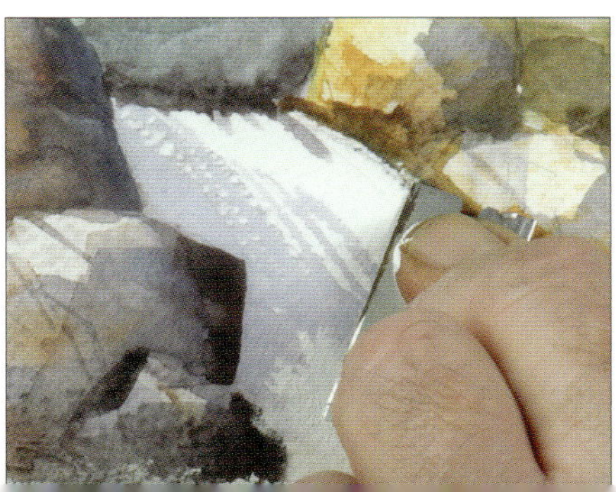

49 Use the razor blade to scrape out some bright highlights on the waterfall after it has dried. Finish your painting by removing any visible pencil lines.

Overleaf

The finished painting.

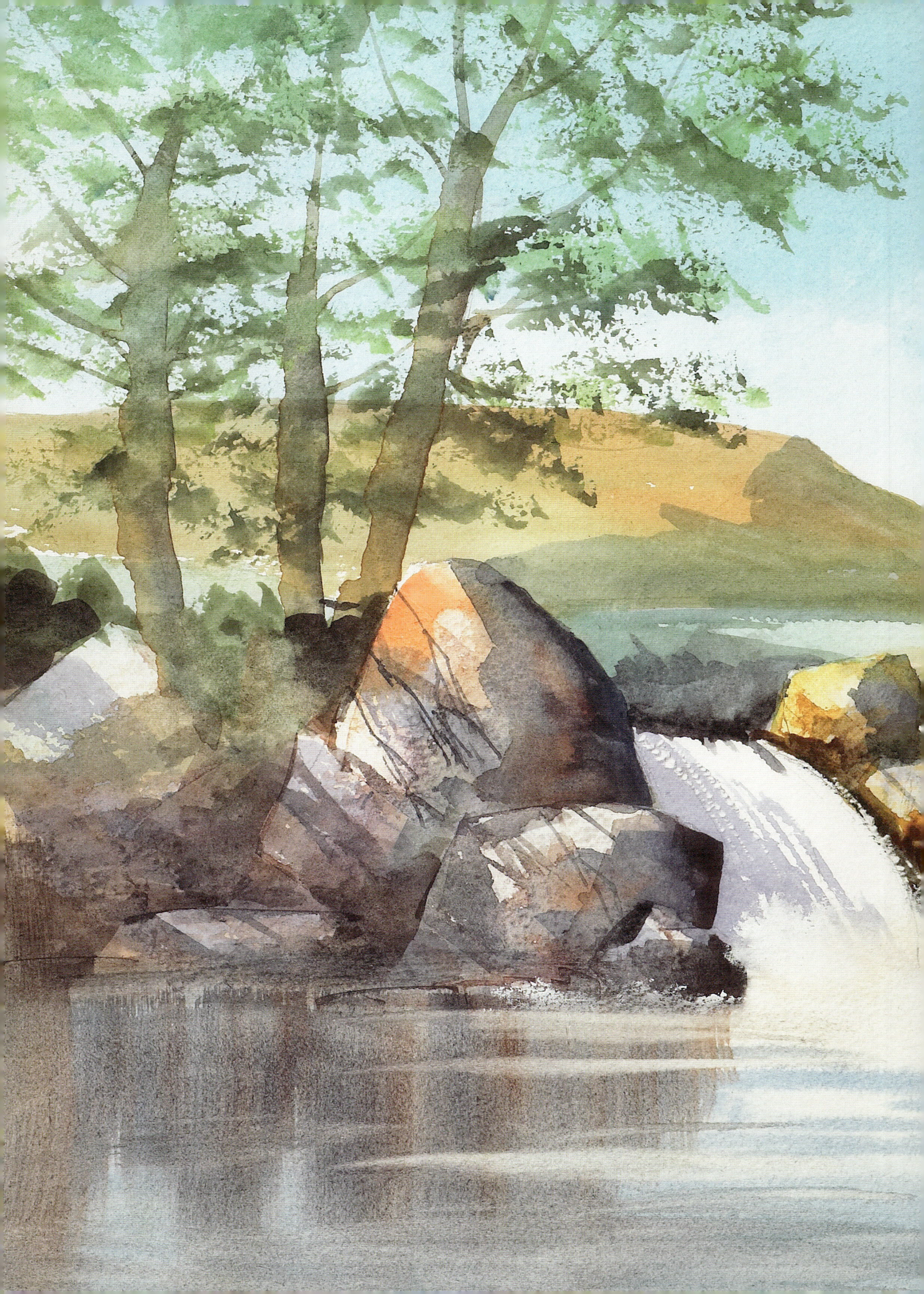

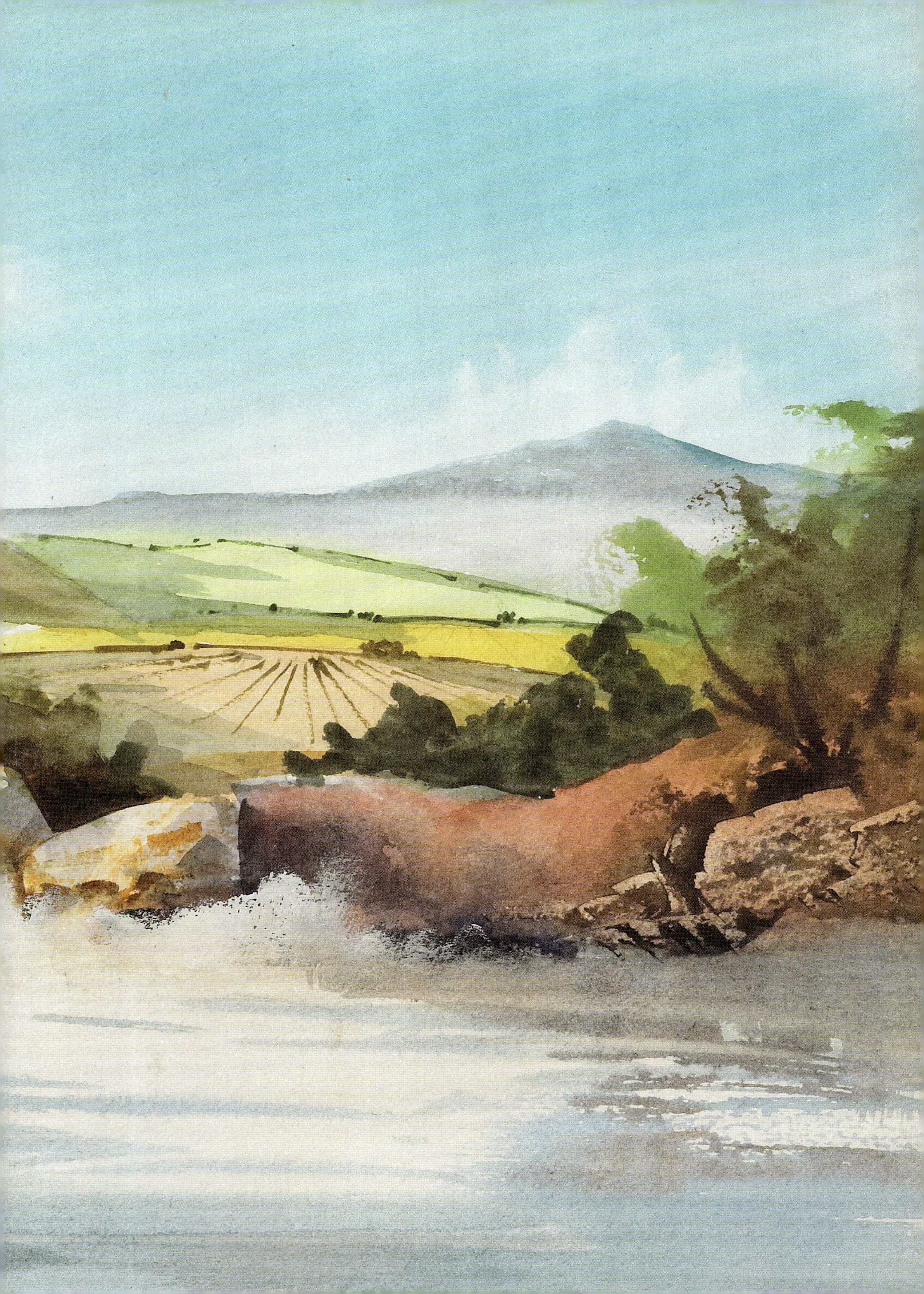

Index

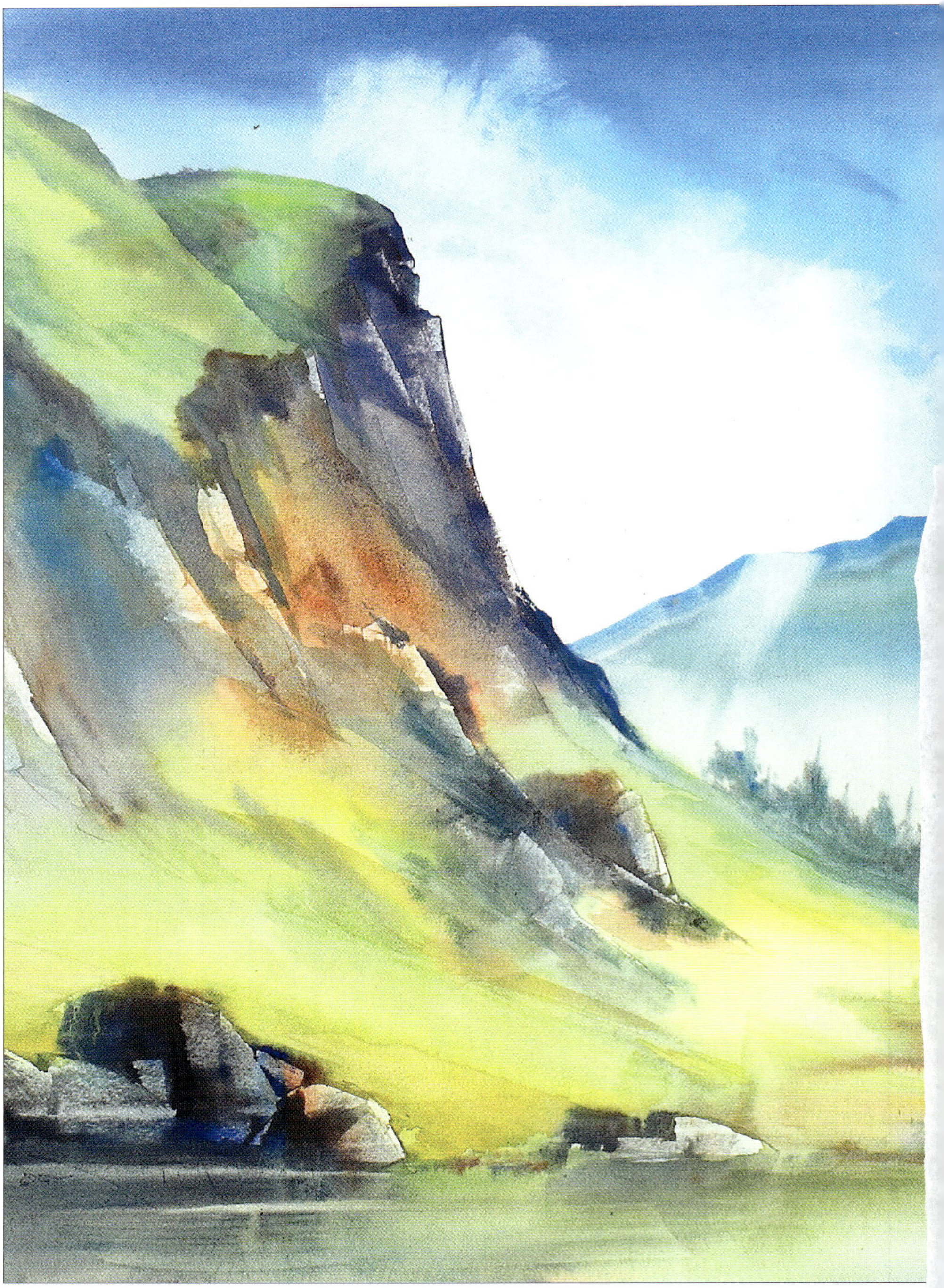